Manifest West

Western Weird

Manifest West

Western Weird

Western
Press Books

WESTERN PRESS BOOKS
GUNNISON, COLORADO

ISBN: 978-1-60732-440-9

Library of Congress Control Number: 2015936938
Published in the United States of America

Western Press Books
Gunnison, Colorado

"Alamo Dreams" appeared in the collection *Let the Birds Drink in Peace* (Conundrum, 2011).

"Blacktop Cuisine" appeared as "America's drive-in—the Roadkill Café," in the *San Francisco Chronicle*, Dec. 2006.

"Genghis' Knoll" appeared in Nate Liederbach's story collection, *Negative Spaces*, published in 2013 by Elik Press, Salt Lake City.

"Cold Night Near Cody" appeared in *Columbia: A Journal of Literature* and *Art 52* (2014).

"Gilapause" appeared in *Southwest Review* 99.2 (2014).

"Laughter Yoga" appeared online in *Ragazine*, Volume 10, Number 6.

"Letter to Josie" appeared in Russell Davis's collection, *The End of All Seasons* (Wildside, 2013).

"New Frontier" appeared in *Handmade History: Poems of the American West* (Bend, Ore.: Two Ravens Publications, 2014).

"Speaking in Tongues" appeared in *Women in Judaism: A Multidisciplinary Journal*, Volume 11:2 (2015).

"Thrown" originally appeared in *Tusculum Review*, issue 1, in 2005; it was reprinted in

Redux in 2012.

"Tunnel of Love" appeared in *Mountainfreak 8* (Spring 1999).

Cover image: SHUTTERSTOCK.COM

EDITOR

MARK TODD

ASSOCIATE EDITORS

LAURA ANDERSON
JENNIFER GAUTHIER
A. J. STERKEL

ASSISTANT EDITORS

REBECCA BISHOP
DONIELLE CARR
M.J. DAU
SARAH FISHER
KANDRA VOLENTINE

CONSULTING EDITOR

LARRY MEREDITH

COVER AND INTERIOR DESIGN

SONYA UNREIN

CONTENTS

THE LEY OF THE LAND

WE ARE NOT ALONE

CONTRIBUTOR NOTES

MARK TODD

Foreword

The 2015 theme for *Manifest West's* annual anthology is Western Weird. The works in this collection reflect both myths and suspected truths about the part of the United States we call The West. But this year's edition focuses entirely on the tradition of the strange. To borrow from Jeff VanderMeer's definition for speculative fiction's New Weird, this volume creates a new parallel genre for work that subverts the traditional romanticized ideas about place, playing with clichés about The West in order to put these elements to discomfiting, rather than consoling, ends.

This fourth edition features thirty-two writers from across the country, but each of them has nonetheless managed to offer work that finds a home in The West. Topics included in this collection of creative nonfiction, poetry, and fiction range from The West's numinous fascination with E.T., Bigfoot, and ghosts to the West's uncomfortable relationships with its own marginalized peoples, with the region's unforgiving and sometimes violent traditions, and with its indigenous fauna and deadly landscapes. The tone of these works ranges from light—even campy—to chilling, but all allow readers to gaze straight into the many faces of what makes The West a weird place.

For the first time in the series, this year's edition includes solicited work as well as open submissions, including a number of established and award-winning writers in addition to its mission of giving voice to both published and brand-new writers.

As we were putting this anthology together, editors discovered how many of the works, regardless of genre, tended to resonate in surprising patterns. To intensify such harmonics, we decided to allow these affinities to determine the sequence of the pieces in this anthology, apportioning the works into the divisions of *The Olden Daze*, *The Ley of the Land*, and *We Are Not Alone*.

Western Weird is the fourth volume in Western Press Books' literary anthology series, *Manifest West*. The press, affiliated with Western State Colorado University, produces one anthology annually, focused on Western regional writing.

We hope you enjoy reading the selections we've chosen as much as we enjoyed collecting them.

THE OLDEN DAZE

RUSSELL DAVIS

FICTION

Letter to Josie

"Now, that's funny." —Doc Holliday

Josephine Marcus Earp
The Oyster Bar
Fifth Avenue
San Diego, California

8 November 1887

Dearest Josie,

It is almost midnight now, and some part of me wants to believe that if I ventured out of my room and downstairs to where the bar is still noisy and the faro tables are still full, I would find him there. He would be sitting in a corner chair, a tumbler of whiskey at his elbow, and a bloodied cloth in his pocket. His sharp blue eyes would be staring down at his cards, and from time to time, a horrible cough would wrack his body. In spite of his illness, he would miss nothing—not a bluff or a tell or a weapon hidden beneath the table. I want to believe this vision, hold it in my heart for as long as I can.

Our lovely John died this morning.

He explained to me that he had seen you and Wyatt last year, in Denver, but I do not know if you have heard from him since. In May of this year, he came here to Glenwood Springs, where I arrived but a few days ago. I had received a letter from him, begging me to come. For all the things that John was in life, he never failed as a gentleman, and coming to him in his last extremity was the least I could do.

5

When I arrived, his first demand was that when it was over I should write to you and Wyatt of his passing and the manner of it. John also felt that it was a matter of some import that you both should be made aware of what truly happened in Fort Griffin, Texas, and how he and Wyatt left there with my gifts, one for each man. I am given to understand that Wyatt himself may be unaware of all this, though it explains much about his life in the years since. As a woman of quality, surely you can understand that sometimes secrets are necessary evils, if for no other reason than to ensure the happiness of our men. And contrary to what has been said publically and elsewise, for a time, John was my man, just as I was his woman.

Still, I am honoring his request. Perhaps it is time that you knew the truth, and if he lacks it, Wyatt himself. On the day of my arrival, once we had managed to dismiss the hovering physician (a man John despised, should you wonder) and that nosy Episcopalian, Rev. Samuel Jefferson (a man John would have happily shot, I should think), I sat down on the edge of his bed and he spoke. "I knew you would come, Carlotta. Other than Josie, you are the only true lady I have known since I came West."

I held his hand and told him that I was happy to be there with him, and he offered me a bloody grin, coughing, and I saw his skeletal frame spasm, but when it passed, he spoke again. "You used to be a much better bluffer, my dear."

It is true that my days at the card table are long behind me now, but it was no matter between friends. He spoke briefly of Fort Griffin, then said, "You may remember that time, when Wyatt and I were there and first met at your faro table. You and that giant nigger woman."

Of course I remembered, though I despised his terminology for my good friend and protector Mary Poindexter. I forgive him that, however, as he was ever a man of the South and some attitudes will never change.

"I certainly recall your words on the night before we left, but if you could illuminate their meaning, dear lady, then I should rest more comfortably in my grave."

"Why?" I asked him, for it seemed a matter of serious importance to him.

"I fear that I may die only to wake once more in this cursed body. I have already died nine times, and I am hopeful that this will be the last, as you once told me."

It is true, Josie, that I predicted that John would be brushed by the hand of Death nine times before he died. Just as I predicted other things that came to pass, for that is my gift and my curse. Alas, my words are racing ahead of events, and I fear that I will only leave you and Wyatt bewildered. It is best that I start at the beginning.

In 1877, I was dealing faro in Fort Griffin at a small, but well-kept place called Shanssey's Saloon, owned by the Irishman of the same name, the man who first introduced our John and Wyatt. At the time, the little town was not far removed from the days of martial law, and many of the elements that made it dangerous still drifted through from time to time: shootists, outlaws, soldiers, gamblers, and no small number of ladies of ill repute called Fort Griffin home, though by that time, it had settled down quite a bit.

In fact, it was John Shanssey himself who first introduced me to John, then Wyatt, and both men gambled at my faro table from time to time. John had drifted in from some trouble elsewhere and in spite of his illness, I was quite taken with him. He was a rare bird in that part of the world—a true gentleman with manners. We had much in common, he and I, and he seemed taken with me. I am a realist, my dear Josie, and I knew that we could never be more than temporary. Still, in that place and in those days, comfort of any kind was a treasure. I saw something in him, something quite unique, but I was unsure of what it was.

Until Wyatt arrived. At that time, Wyatt was hunting a somewhat infamous train robber by the name of Dave Rudabaugh. He'd trailed him for four hundred miles and came into Shanssey's looking as worn as a dead cowboy's boot. He was dirty from head to toe with the dust and grime of the chase, but after speaking to Shannsey, he came directly over to where John was sitting and explained who he was looking for and that it was his understanding that John and Rudabaugh had played cards recently.

John looked up at Wyatt and said, "We did, indeed. And while I don't normally associate with lawmen and their causes, I would be remiss if I did not encourage your efforts, for Rudabaugh is the lowest kind of scoundrel."

Wyatt took a chair at the table and said—in that voice of his, so low and even that each word has a timbre of its own, "What kind of scoundrel is that?"

"A cheater at cards and a liar in public," John replied. "Were it not for my recent vow to . . . avoid unpleasantness, I might have saved you the time."

"You have something of a reputation yourself, Mr. Holliday," Wyatt said.

"I have heard of you as well, Wyatt Earp. You can call me Doc."

Wyatt got to his feet and said, "Thanks for your time, Mr. Holliday."

I thought then that it was over, but something quite unexpected happened. John reached out and put his hand on Wyatt's arm and said, "Rudabaugh headed back north, toward Kansas. If you catch up to him, shoot him once for me."

Wyatt smiled that grim smile of his and said, "If I catch up to him, he'll be jailed. After that, his fate will be up to the judge and the jury."

"I had heard you were the killing kind." John looked him up and down. "I can see it on you as easily as I see the dust on your coat."

"I have heard some stories about you, too, Mr. Holliday."

The second those words left his mouth, the sight came upon me. "You two," I told them, "are going to be the fastest of friends. You will save each other's lives many times over."

"There aren't many men I would call friend," John said.

"Nor I," Wyatt said.

I stood and poured each of them a tumbler of whiskey. "Gentlemen, this future is already writ in the heavens."

John took his tumbler and held it out to Wyatt and said, "To not being friends, then."

"To not being friends," he replied.

They drank, and that was the beginning of what happened in Fort Griffin, Josie. Before I can tell you the rest of it, I believe I shall adjourn downstairs and have a drink myself. In honor of John and to steel my nerves. You may wish to have one yourself before you read on, my dear, though all the whiskey in the world will not wash away the truth of my words, but it might prepare you to believe them.

* * *

My birth name, as you may well know, was Carlotta Thompkins, though I have had many names in the years since. I say without any pride that I have been called the Angel of San Antonio, the Queen of the Pasteboards, and most famously, Lottie Deno. The name that was most accurate, though only one person truly knew it at the time, was Mystic Maud.

My caretaker Mary Poindexter, whom I have mentioned, was a family slave when I was born. Assigned to my care, she served as protector and companion, and her height—which neared seven feet—was as intimidating as the power in her eyes. She also taught me to use my gift, which has served me well in building a life for myself. My gift, as you may have guessed, is that of precognition. It is not a burden I would recommend, and without Mary's help, surely the visions that have plagued me throughout my life would have driven me mad. As it was, she helped me to see more clearly what the future held for myself and sometimes others, and to block the vision out when it would do more harm than good to see what was to come.

I tell you all this, Josie, to help you understand what it was I saw in John and Wyatt that day. I foresaw them becoming fast friends, yes, but there was much more and this part of the story is known only to those of us who were there—myself, Mary, Wyatt, John, and three men who'd ridden into Fort Griffin the same day as Wyatt called the Bentmoots brothers, whose names were Billy, Isaac, and Frank. I'd heard when they came into town from one of the girls at the mercantile, who said she'd seen them and that they gave her a sick feeling in the pit of her stomach.

This was in the wintertime, and business was often slow during the week-nights. Shanssey had left the bar in my hands for the night, and as my only two customers were Wyatt and John, the three of us sat together, drinking and talking quietly, playing faro or poker to pass the time. Outside, the winds blew cold and kept the streets empty, at least until the Bentmoots came in.

From the looks of them, they were hard cases. You certainly know the type. They wore long, tattered dusters and their hats were pulled low over their eyes. And if I noticed that their weapons were well used and the leather of their holsters worn smooth, then I harbor no doubt that both John and Wyatt saw the same things in them. But there was something about these men that was different. All three of us saw it, I think, though if pressed, it would have been difficult to name whatever it was that made them different.

The three sat down, never removing their dusters or their hats, taking chairs across the table from John and Wyatt. The one in the middle spoke, and his voice was a low, growling croak. "Whiskey all around."

I poured and the three men drank, then he said in a voice that remained unchanged by the lubrication, "We'd play a hand of cards with you Doc Holliday and Wyatt Earp. One hand of poker, for old time's sake."

"I do not know you," Wyatt said.

"Neither do I," John added.

"But we know you," he said. "I'm Frank Bentmoots. This is Billy and Isaac. One hand and then we'll be on our way. The moon is rising with the wind."

Wyatt began to shake his head, but John cleared his throat and put his money clip on the table. "How much?" he asked. I heard the change in his voice that told me he was about to be dangerous, but I wasn't sure why.

"Not money," Frank said. "One hand for all the marbles." He reached into his duster pocket and pulled out a handful of chips. "One chip for each and every one. The person who wins the hand gets them all."

John held out his hand to inspect them. "The Oriental," he said. "I do not believe I am familiar with the establishment."

"You will be," Frank growled. "Are you in or out?"

Putting his money back into his vest, John said, "I'm in, and so is Wyatt. Five card draw."

"I didn't agree to that, Doc," he said, by now using the familiar name. "Something's not right here."

"I feel lucky," he replied.

Wyatt shrugged. "One chip for each man at the table, the rest in the center. Lottie here will deal."

"Done," Frank said, handing out a single chip to each man and giving the rest to the pot. "But don't you be cheatin', Holliday!"

"I never cheat," he said, looking at me. "Deal them straight, Lottie."

I shuffled the deck and dealt the hand. Five cards to each man. John never touched his, but left them on the table. The man furthest to my left, Billy, asked for three. Frank asked for two. Isaac for four. Wyatt asked for two, looking at his hand in disgust and at the strange men with unease. John's turn came and he shook his head. "None for me," he said. His voice was quiet and filled with venom.

"None?" Frank growled in disbelief. "You didn't even look at them. Show your cards!"

John shook his head. "Same order as the deal."

Billy flipped over his cards, showing a pair of jacks.

"You next, Isaac," Frank said. "I'll wait."

Isaac turned his cards over, and had a broken straight.

"Go ahead, Wyatt," John said.

Wyatt revealed his hand. Three of a kind tens.

Frank laughed and it was a sound I never wanted to hear again. "You're doomed, Holliday," he said. He showed his hand, which was a king high spade flush. "Show your cards."

John nodded and flipped them over one by one. The first two cards were aces, and as he turned over and revealed the third ace, I heard the wind pick up outside and saw in the way I do that this was going to end in violence. He paused, his precise fingers lingering over the fourth card, then turning it upright and revealing the last ace.

Frank surged to his feet. "You're a damn cheat, Holliday! There's no way you pulled that blind!"

John never moved, but simply said, in that slow way of his, "Prove it."

Before anyone could react, Frank lunged across the table and flipped over John's fifth card. It, too, was an ace. As his eyes lit on the card, Frank's hand pulled his gun. It was halfway clear of the leather when Wyatt's gun sounded.

Billy and Isaac both jumped up and drew, but Wyatt fired twice more, killing them both.

John looked at the carnage and smiled. "I do believe he caught me cheating."

"What's your game, Doc?" Wyatt said. "I just killed those men."

"And they stink to the heavens," John replied, getting to his feet and making his way over to the bodies. Wyatt and I moved with him and to our surprise, all three of them had the appearance of men long dead—their flesh was grayish-green and rotting, sloughing off the bones of their faces, their nails were curled and cracked and dirty. As we watched, the wind grew outside to a shriek, then the door flew open and as the grit from outside swirled around us, the three men simply dried up and disappeared. There was nothing left of any of them.

Stunned, we sat back down at the table.

"Carlotta, pour us a round, if you please," John said.

I did and we sat in silence for several long minutes.

Wyatt finally spoke. "I don't . . . I knew something wasn't right . . ." Words failed him then.

John said, "I don't know who or what they were, ghosts maybe, as I have heard of such things, but I guessed that something was amiss."

"How?" I asked him.

"Because of the chips," he said, gathering them up one by one. "There are many saloons and gaming halls across this part of the world, and some may even be called the Oriental, but I do know one thing." He held the chip up so I could see it. "There is no Tombstone, Arizona. If there were, surely I would have a place there by now."

Wyatt laughed, somewhat weakly. "Why didn't you draw your gun, Doc?"

"Because I knew you would," he said, trying not to cough. "You *are* the killing kind, Wyatt."

My vision came upon me then, Josie, and I saw more of what the future held for these two men. I couldn't bring myself to tell them all of it, so I settled for giving one bit of foresight to them each. A gift, as I saw it, to give them hope for the many dark days they would face ahead.

To John I said, "Nine times in your life, you will be touched by Death and nine times you will best him. Four times from the hangman's noose and five times from the gun. Stay near Wyatt and be true, and when Death comes for you the tenth time, it will be from natural causes."

To Wyatt I said, "For so long as you remain a true friend of John Holliday, you will be untouched by bullet or knife, but Death will ride with you as a companion for many years. You will find true love in an unexpected place and your fame will be writ large for all the world to see."

I couldn't tell them the rest. I didn't have the heart.

You know the rest of their story, my dear Josie. And you know what happened in Tombstone, which was founded that same year that Wyatt and John first met there in Fort Griffin. What you don't know, and they certainly didn't, was that the three men who came for them that night were not ghosts from the past, but from the future. Bentmoots is simply a rearrangement of the letters in Tombstone, and the names Frank McClaury, Billy Claibourne, and Isaac Clanton are already familiar to you.

Somehow, those dead men from the future found their way back to the past.

And for some reason, they believed they could win back their future with a single hand of poker against one of the greatest gamblers of his time. It may have helped that I dealt him the four aces, but the fifth one was entirely his doing.

I doubt they ever spoke of it again. Men have a way of forgetting the unexplainable, just as women have a way of forgiving the unforgivable. All I know is that the future I saw in them that dark, cold night in Fort Griffin came true, and this morning, John Holliday woke for the last time.

He asked for a drink of whiskey, which I gave him, looked down at his naked feet and said, "Now, that's funny," and died. I imagine he believed he would die with his boots on.

Share this letter with Wyatt, or not, as you choose, but tell him . . . tell the world . . .

Doc Holliday is dead.

> Yours most sincerely,
> Carlotta Thompkins

BARTHOLOMEW BRINKMAN

Dinosaur National Monument

Florescent pink Triceratops
and orange Pterodactyls guard
the roadside inns where we would swim
in overchlorinated pools,

replenish ice from down the hall
and for a couple quarters quake
the unsuspecting waterbeds
in wave after undulating wave.

But we came here mostly to see the quarry,
chiseled deep in the distant Uintahs,
where inch by glaciating inch,
a grotesque mural has unfurled

itself unto the world,
excavating lost remains
of brittle bones long turned to stone,
and dusting the dry beds for prints.

I knew the lot of them already—
Allosaur, Triceratops,
the Great Tyrannosaurus Rex.
I'd recognize their shapes

as surely as I knew my shadow
burning into the soft tar
of an early afternoon
in the empty streets of summer.

Those certain skeletal frames contort
beneath the heft of hulking skulls,
teeth as big as hammer heads,
sockets deep as trouser pockets,

trunks, like trucks stuck in the mud,
ridged ribs like bridges collapsing
into themselves in a flood
of sudden devastation.

But as I stood there, peering over
the precipice, face to face
with that steep, unscalable cliff—
that impossibly deep chasm—

opening his gaping mouth
how could he articulate
without succumbing to
these cataclysmic spasms?

My mother held me tightly
as I stared into the future,
keeping me from stumbling over
the sudden edge of understanding.

DANIEL ERVIN

The Buddha's Geology

There are still leaves
now. But they're changing too quickly,
falling faster than water over rock,
dying like a thought in a late night.
I'm walking, eyes fixed forward
on nothing, guessing which leaves the next gust of wind will take.

The wind breathes and the bits of autumn it takes
are only those which I did not see—not the leaves
I expected to move. I walk forward
into the urgent uncertainty of change. It's quick,
unwilling to calm itself while I peer into the night-
lit future. The wind takes leaves. Its work is slower on rock.

Far away, the wind is talking to a rock
in Nebraska. A rock whose steady journey has taken
it under seas and rivers, trampled it under a million moon-lit nights
through an eon where a leaf
was a distant rumor, spoken of in quick
whispers. The rock relies on wind to move forward.

Forward! shout the heavens. Forward!
Someone in a car down the road listens to music. Rock,
I think. I imagine two nervous lovers, kissing quickly,
ruing a missed opportunity, lamenting a ride not taken.
Rolling through whorls of dirt on the street and crunching autumn leaves
they drive, each casting longing furtive glances at the other and all around
   them, the night.

Slowly, run slowly, horses of the night.
But they won't. They charge forward
with me and the stars and the sun and leaves
and the seasons and the mountain (now only a little rock)
in tow. Stand and be taken.
The night will be no longer for your longing—do not go too quickly.

My consciousness is quickening,
congealing like wind caught in a mountainous night.
The chill wind whispers a *suscipe*—"Take,
leaves, and receive all my energy." Forward
ride the horses. Changing forever is the rock,
and the body is always either growing or decaying before it leaves.
My mind's ferocity decays. Even rotting, it propels the universe forward.
The fleeting night has come to an understanding with the rock.
The nature of all things takes the clothing off my brain.
Everything dies. Nothing leaves.

FICTION

Cheater

I held my pepperbox pistol beneath the card table and aimed at the head of the cheating cowboy. "You know eight cards in five card stud is called a 'dead man's hand' don't you?"

'Twasn't hard to see his hand held eight cards, and we were playing five card stud! He made a move. I pulled the trigger. The bullet hit him under the chin and exited the top of his head, followed by what brains he had. The saloon filled with silence as I stood up and walked to where he fell. All eyes were on me as he lay at my feet, blood pouring from his wound. Then the same pairs of eyes all looked the other way. None wanted to be a witness to a shooting.

I gathered my winnings off the table and hit the trail to the next town before some do-gooder tried to get me locked up for killing someone's son, husband, or father. Emotional relatives often overlooked the fact that their loved ones got caught cheating.

I had won enough to get myself a little business. Tired of gambling and killing, I headed for Denver, the biggest burg in Colorado, looking for an opportune investment. I'd been traveling and gambling since the war ended in '65. My aim in life now was to settle down, hang up my guns, and never look at a deck of cards again.

The mountains were just turning green, but snow still topped most peaks in the Rockies. I knew I'd best keep an eye out for hungry grizzlies this time of year. When I reached town, I rode down the main street and saw people beginning to gather around a man who talked in a voice loud enough to echo up and down the dusty lane. With promises of easy money, he soon drew a crowd. He set up his "tripe and keister," a display case on a tripod, on the wooden sidewalk.

"All right, folks, step right up. My name's Soapy Smith and I'm gonna make you an incredible offer you can't refuse." He held up a bar of soap.

Hell, I knew cowboys only needed that once a year or so. How he'd make money selling soap piqued my curiosity, though, so I clambered off my horse to hang around and watch. He placed ordinary, rectangular, homemade cakes of soap onto the keister top, and he began to expound on their wonders. As he spoke to the curious onlookers, he pulled out a roll of bills and began to wrap paper money around a few cakes of soap. He used notes ranging from one dollar up to one hundred dollars. Then he finished his handiwork by wrapping plain brown paper around each cake of soap and mixed the money-wrapped bars in with the plain ones.

"Cleanliness is next to Godliness, but the feel of a good crisp greenback in the pocket is paradise itself. Step up, my friends, and buy some heaven-scented soap to please your ladies for one measly dollar. You just might make a ninety-nine dollar profit when you peel the wrapping off," he shouted.

I watched a man, who I figured to be a shill planted in the crowd, buy a cake. He tore it open and loudly proclaimed that he'd won some money, waving it around for all to see. The shill looked enough like Soapy to be his brother.

This performance had the desired effect. The crowd clamored to buy the soap for one dollar a cake. I laughed as some of the victims bought several cakes before the sale was completed. Another shill hollered in excitement when he tore the wrappings off the soap he had bought and showed the crowd the note wrapped around the soap.

Soapy Smith announced that the hundred-dollar note yet remained in the pile. He started to auction off the remaining soap and the highest bidder could choose which one he wanted. My carefully trained eye had seen his manipulation and sleight-of-hand. I stepped forward. "If I win the auction, I can choose any cake of soap I want, is that correct?"

"You can choose any soap I have if you win."

Soapy Smith started the auction. I got my choice for seven dollars and fifty cents, a royal sum. The crowd watched in suspense as I approached, pointed to his right side jacket pocket where I saw him stash the cake he had wrapped with the hundred-dollar note. He attempted to do the old switcheroo once more, but I grabbed his soap-filled hand, reached into his pocket and withdrew the soap. I unwrapped it in front of the crowd to show them the money. Once they saw I had won the big one, they quit bidding and walked away. Not a one demanded their money back. I figured they must be scared of this hombre for some reason.

"I'll get you for this," Soapy Smith mumbled in my direction.

I looked him dead in the eye, ready to draw both my hidden pistols. "No time like the present," I snarled.

He could tell I wasn't bluffing. He packed his keister, folded his tripe, and strode away muttering threats under his breath. I tied up my mount and sauntered into the Elite Saloon and Hotel where I rented a room and a tub full of hot water. I paid with the crisp $100 bill, and I put the cake of soap to good use. Had a meal in the dining room, and then I slept until sunbeams shining through the grime-covered window woke me.

Feeling refreshed after the meal, the bath, and the long sleep, I headed downstairs where I knew a poker game would be in progress. Sure enough, before I hit the bottom step I spotted a table occupied by five men playing seven-card stud. I grabbed an empty chair, pulled it to the table, and sat.

Out of the five, four were cowboys, but the fifth I recognized from the day before. He was the first shill in the crowd to buy soap from Soapy Smith. Today he was dressed as a cardsharp in his costume of black jacket, trousers, and hat decorated with silver studs. His bolo tie, tipped in gold with a gold nugget for a slide, showed off his prosperity. When I caught his eye, I tipped my hat.

He tipped his in return. "Bascomb Smith here," he said.

Definitely Soapy's brother. Cooking up a card scheme, no doubt.

An older, distinguished-looking gentleman who held the deck ready to deal nodded at me. "Ante's five dollars, high card bets, twenty-dollar limit on raises."

"Percival Morse," I said, and threw my five dollars into the pot.

The dealer started tossing cards. "I'm Bradley Broome, the barber and undertaker in this here town."

The other four didn't say a word, just watched Brad's hands as he dealt the cards. Time passed and the game progressed. Slowly, I began to acquire a substantial amount of their money. The players were making snide remarks to each other about me being a dude with my clean white shirt, something they didn't see very often. They figured me as a dude, and any dude had to be stupid. Most cowboys wouldn't think I'd be brave enough or smart enough to cheat them. I was both and cheated them out of their gold every chance I got.

One of the players, Billy, had been smashed in the head with an Indian tomahawk some years ago. The tomahawk must've scrambled his brains—he played and talked like a half-wit, but his money was good.

Smith's hand showed aces and eights. He bet all the coins and bills piled in front of him. To match his bet I had to use my entire take and the lucky twenty-dollar gold piece I'd carried all through the war. I rubbed it hard before I threw it on the table. Smith held three hole cards, and the aces and eights in his hand would have turned into four aces when he added the two I saw him pull from his sleeve. These young whippersnappers thought because they could handle a deck of cards smoothly, no one could catch their shenanigans. Darn stupid cowboys, they all think I can't spot a card cheat. But they better learn to cheat good, or don't cheat at all.

This pot turned out to be the biggest my eyes had beheld in a long time. I had two kings showing and two in the hole. I wasn't going to let someone beat my kickers with palmed aces.

I shot Smith smack in the middle of his forehead. His eyes opened wide in surprise, and as the light drained from them, he tried to stand but fell to the floor. I wasn't about to let anybody cheat me out of my lucky coin.

I held my four-shot pepperbox pistol aimed at the other players while I gathered my winnings from the table. I had three shots left in the pepperbox and under my left sleeve, another seven shots in my .22 Rimfire revolver. Billy the half-wit grabbed my lucky twenty-dollar gold piece from the table and put it in his mouth.

"Spit it out, Billy, or you'll lay beside Smith." I looked at Smith's body laid out on the floor and Billy's eyes followed mine. "I'm going to count to three, and if that gold piece isn't on the table, you're going to have a hole in your head to match his." I put the pepperbox against his forehead. I couldn't believe he'd give up his life for twenty bucks. His eyes dared me to shoot. I squeezed the trigger and a small bloodless hole appeared in his forehead. He slumped back in his chair. I didn't want to do it, but I couldn't let him call my bluff. If I did, I'd be dead meat in minutes.

I gazed around the table to warn those still alive they wouldn't be for long if they did anything stupid like Billy. I tried to open his mouth to retrieve the twenty-dollar gold coin, but I couldn't get it to open.

"Locks up like a safe when they die biting down on something," Brad said.

"What are you talking about?"

"I'm telling you when someone dies biting down on something their jaws lock. The only way you'll get that gold piece is to break his jaw loose. I know what I'm talking about. I've had to break many a jaw to make their faces look normal for viewing and picture taking."

I swung the butt of my gun against Billy's jaw and heard the bone crack. He toppled from the chair to the ground. I stooped down and tried forcing his jaw opened with my free hand. "Don't make a move," I warned them and put the barrel of my pepperbox between Billy's lips and fired. That's one way to force a mouth open. I laughed and shot a look at the undertaker.

"Didn't do much good, did it?" the undertaker said.

I looked at Billy and there was a hole blown through his lips and teeth, but his jaws were still locked. I put my gun to the undertaker's head. "You know how. Open his jaws and get my gold out of his mouth."

I watched as he put one hand on the cadaver's head and one on the jaw. He twisted hard in opposite directions. Then he repeated the procedure by twisting them back and forth. I heard a loud snap, but he still couldn't get the mouth open to retrieve my lucky piece.

A figure plowed through the swinging doors, guns in hand, ready to shoot someone. "Bascomb," Soapy cried out when he saw Billy lying on the floor with a spreading puddle of blood around his head. His eyes burned with hatred as he spotted me. "You! First you rob me, now you've kilt my brother. You're going to pay and pay big." His guttural voice turned to tears as he holstered his guns and bent over his brother.

Pitiful, a grown man crying. I should have shot him then, but I didn't have it in me to shoot a crying man. I hated to leave my lucky piece in the mouth of a dead half-wit, but I knew I better skedaddle before help for Soapy arrived. I gathered my winnings and rode hard.

My horse headed toward Colorado Springs, but that town was said to be awfully refined and devoid of liquor, so I stopped for supplies in Colorado City.

I spotted a wanted poster with my image on the front of the town marshall's office declaring a reward of five hundred dollars, dead or alive. I ripped the poster from the wall. Five hundred dollars would get a lot of people hunting for me. I knew I'd better change my appearance. I slunk away, wandering until I found a general store and traded in my matching pants and jacket for cowboy duds. My shoes were replaced by a fine pair of sculptured boots. I decided not to shave for a long time. With any luck, no one would recognize me as the same man on the wanted poster.

Over twenty years had passed since the gold strike at Pikes Peak, but there was still plenty of loose gold floating around in the saloons. I figured I'd have time to play some poker before I moved on. I went to the best hotel in Colorado City, the Hoffman Hotel, a hole in the wall by the grand standards of Colorado Springs, and rented a room for a week. Right upstairs, the Hoffman Saloon bustled twenty-four hours a day. There I found four cowboys playing a game of five-card draw poker. They eyeballed my starchy new clothes, but cowboys usually buy a new outfit when the old one wears out, so they welcomed me as one of their own.

As usual, I began to accumulate the money bet back and forth, small change for me. These were working cowboys, and only earned thirty dollars a month, so it didn't take long before all four were out of cash.

"One more hand," one of the cowboys said.

"Sure. Put up your ante if you want to play."

"I'll put up my brand new gun," he said. "It's a new style .44 Colt. Packs enough power to kill a grizzly, if you hit it between the eyes."

I threw up twenty silver dollars against his gun. "Five card stud. Just turn them all face up, no bets or raises."

He smiled when his first card was an ace and mine, a deuce. He got a jack and another deuce landed in front of me. His next card gave him a pair of aces and he smiled again as I got a three of clubs. We watched each other warily as he was dealt another jack. I got a four of diamonds. He had a big smile on now, anticipating how he would spend the twenty. When the last round fell, he got a ten of spades and I another deuce.

As soon as he saw the third deuce, he grabbed the gun from the table and trained it on me. "Get his gun," he told his buddy.

The buddy came up behind me and relieved me of both my weapons, then struggled to remove the wad of cash from my rear pocket.

But a shot rang out. Soapy stood by the door with his pistol smoking. "Stand back, he's mine. I'm taking him back to Denver where he's going to hang for killing my brother."

He strode to the cowboy who pointed the .44 at me and removed it from his hand. Scooping up the twenty silver dollars with one hand, he gave them to the cowboy. "For your .44, now git."

We headed toward Denver with me tied to my saddle like a sack of potatoes. I started saying my prayers. I knew if Soapy got me that far, it was all over. But Providence intervened and sent a powerful rainstorm with thunder and lightning that crashed through the mountains and spooked the horses. We found a cave, but the horses wouldn't enter. After dismounting, Soapy untied me from the saddle but left my hands tied together. He tethered both horses to a tree, and we ran for the cave.

A bear smell told us a bear lived there—that probably spooked the horses as much as the storm.

"Nothing pisses a grizzly bear off more than someone entering its den. I'm putting you between the opening and me while I get some sleep. If the bear comes back while I'm sleeping, it'll eat you, not me." Soapy laughed and slapped his thigh.

Soapy tied me with the lariat he pulled from his saddlebag. I looked at his holster and saw the new .44 in it. He left me lying on the cold damp cave floor between him and the opening. He stretched out by the fire and fell asleep with the .44 on his chest.

Bear bait for Soapy and not much I could do about it. When he began to snore, I began to pick at the knots he'd tied me up with, the bear in mind all the while. If he shot at the bear and missed, it would only piss it off. But not many could shoot as straight as me. These thoughts encouraged me to work harder on untying those knots. Once the first knot unraveled, the rest of the knots came undone easier.

I stared at Soapy with that .44 lying on his chest. My legs shook and my belly froze up as I crawled over the cold damp ground to his sleeping form. Sweat dripped from every pore, even in the chilly air. Finally, I scooted up beside him and slowly reached for the gun. My hand was on it when we both heard a grumbling roar.

The grizzly had gotten a whiff of us. I quickly grabbed the gun and aimed it at Soapy.

Soapy sat up and uttered a not so funny laugh. "I figured you might try something like that, so I emptied it." He opened his big right hand. Six .44 cartridges rested in his calloused palm. I shook violently now. That bear crept forward. I had to deal both with it *and* Soapy, and no way I could do either with an empty gun.

Soapy stood and stretched above me with his considerable height. "Percival Morse, give me my gun back and I'll take it easy on you when I beat the crap out of you for taking it."

The bear growled and then roared, lunging forward in a way that made me jump back.

"Give me that damn gun and I'll tell the law not to hang you," Soapy said, raw fear quivering in his voice.

I refused. The bear was close now. It couldn't yet see us because of the fire's glare, but we both knew what would happen once it could.

Soapy began to plead in his best shyster, soap-selling voice. "Please. Before the bear goes past the fire." His shaking hands betrayed his quiet words.

I again refused. "Give me the bullets so I can shoot the bear."

"And once you shoot the bear, you'll turn around and shoot me."

"I'm not giving you the gun," I said, as another roar poured from the beast.

Soapy and I stared at each other.

"All right, I'll give you one bullet to shoot the bear with." Soapy tossed one to me, which I hurriedly loaded into the gun and aimed it at him

"What're you doing?" he yelled. "Shoot the bear, you fool."

"I think I'll shoot you to get the rest of the bullets for the bear."

Soapy's hand went to his mouth. I pulled the trigger, and a round hole appeared between his eyes just as he locked his jaws around the bullets.

That's cheating, I thought.

I closed my eyes as I felt the bear's steamy, berry-scented breath on my face . . .

BREDT BREDTHAUER

Hallelujah and Praise Sam Houston

I was born just south of Crawfish Cove,
only child of an immigrant and a cowboy

preacher. I lived with a mosquito in my right ear
and read Keats in a schoolyard bustling with cactus.

I remember the sun
looked like a used condom.

Indian paintbrushes were Confederate flags.
Blue jays sang Baptist hymns while building

nests in the juniper and mesquite.
In that southern heat, we survived

by injecting Florida oranges with Jim Beam
and drinking malt liquor from hollow pumpkins.

FICTION

Alamo Dreams

My wife and I ride horses somewhere in the southwest, along with thirty or forty men. I'm in charge, it appears. Ride up that hill, boys, I say, and my wife glances over approvingly. Hey, you, you're doing good, she seems to be saying.

We're young. It's in the early years of our marriage, and the kids haven't been born yet, but in a way we already have them; they're just waiting to make their move. They're out there somewhere, like shadows, like happy ghosts, ready to spring out of the sagebrush and join us on the ride.

The horses kick up dirt as they scramble up the brown, cactus-strewn hill, and we sense danger and take cover behind the boulders. We don't see the enemy yet, but we know the enemy is close.

My wife has a sunburned nose and reddish-blonde hair trailing out beneath her cowboy hat. She's in her early twenties, just as she was when we met, but I also feel the weight of years in her face, as if she has already lived out our thirty years together, as if even in dreams time can't be cheated.

For the moment, our group is feeling good to be in cover, but I feel sorry for the others. They don't know we're headed for the Alamo. They don't know we're all doomed. It's a warm spring afternoon, the birds are chirping, we're in good cover, and we're armed. We're checking over our guns here and we've gotten a good deal. We've got six-shooters instead of old cap-and-ball muskets. But then three things happen quickly, one good, two bad.

The good thing is that just as we're getting bored and hot on the hill, we shift location into a beautiful canyon. We're on an island in the middle of a clear, cold lake, and we chuckle, all the boys and my wife and me. We chuckle over our good fortune to be in this beautiful place with all the fresh water. There's no way the enemy can cut off our water supply, and there's no way they can surprise us.

The boys get rowdy and boisterous, wading in the water, splashing each other, and ripping off their shirts to show off their chests to my wife. But I hold back. I see clouds moving over the rim of the canyon, shadows falling on the island. My wife sits on a rock next to me and she looks over and says, low, so the others won't hear: We're headed for the Alamo, aren't we?

I'm sorry, I say.

She shivers. She's always known somehow. From the first moment we met, when she looked into my eyes, she knew if she hooked up with me, we'd be headed for the Alamo. We'd ride there together.

The first bad thing that happens is that the enemy appears. Initially, we only glimpse a few shadowy figures on the rim of the canyon, there for a moment, then disappearing. Did we even see them? The men call out in alarm: *Did you see something?* The men argue, convince themselves they didn't see anything, that it was just the sun gleaming. They're trying to go back to their fun when the whole rim of the canyon fills with thousands of blue-shirted soldiers.

From above, they open fire on us, and we realize what a pathetic, puny little force we are, crawling about on the rocks like lizards, scrambling for shelter from the hail of bullets. Now the island doesn't seem like a refuge, but a deathtrap.

My wife glances at me. Sweat beads over her lip. Fire back! I order the men.

But now we discover the second bad thing. Our good repeaters are gone. We're back to old muskets and our powder is wet. The guns melt and droop like taffy. Our guns blow up and send our men flying backwards like cartoon characters. My wife and I work side by side, cramming down our ramrods, firing up at the rim of the canyon, though the bullets fly out in slow motion and drop into the lake.

The lake fills with enemy boats paddling toward the island.

Retreat, I yell, retreat! I grab my wife's hand and we plunge through brush and fall, upwards it seems, and come to our feet in the Alamo. It's not an old fort or a mission, but a ruined mansion, pitted with holes in the walls and ceilings.

It's just before dawn, and quiet. Candles flicker. Sentries are posted at the top and bottom of a great winding stairway.

My wife and I wander through the smoky, once elegant mansion.

Colonel Travis, exhausted looking but stylish in a waistcoat even after days of siege, appears and takes us aside into a secluded corner of the mansion.

Our eyes meet amidst the flickering light. He's young, handsome, intense.

Tell me honestly, he says, is this the Alamo?

My wife and I exchange glances, nod slowly.

He lowers his head. A tremor passes through his chest and shoulders before he looks up at us and says: No help is coming, is it?

He looks about at the men guarding the mansion. A sentry calls from the top of the stairway, Looks all clear, sir!

They don't know yet, Travis whispers to us. Then there's nothing, nothing we can do . . .

Colonel, my wife says. How's the ammunition?

He looks at her as if taking her in for the first time, her sunburned nose, her long blonde hair, the gravity in her youthful face. Low, he whispers, the ammunition is low.

We'll go for more, she says.

He nods. Good. Do what you can. Find your way out of here.

The sentry at the top of the stairway cries out, falls and rolls down the stairs.

To the ramparts! Travis orders.

It's chaos then, fire and smoke and explosions. I discover an old pirate's sword in my hand and I slash it through the air, creating a path as my wife and I run through the swirl of clashing bodies. We run through a dark corridor and out of the flaming mansion and into a parking lot where we hop into a red Mazda, the first car we ever owned.

As we drive through a fierce rain, I crack open a beer.

DON KUNZ

New Frontier

Three centuries of pushing westward,
We are guided at last to Oregon's edge,
Hard dark volcanic headlands anchored
By stunted pine, beach plum, sea grass.
Tide pools mirror the haggard faces
We now find haunting our clawed
Nightmares, scuttling into rocky crevices:
Lynched slaves dangling like bruised fruit;
Railroads crossing our manifest destiny,
Like whipped scars on coolies' backs;
Our fertile fields broken into dust;
Tribes murdered, their feathers in our caps.

Here green grows gray, solid liquid, past now.
Beyond crusted sea-stack monuments,
Breakers arise like grumbling apparitions,
Rolling, roiling, rumpling the misty Pacific,
Bearing the churning energy of future storms,
Burying our blistered feet in sea foam shocking,
Cold, bitter, without the balm of myth.
Far beyond the ravenous, sucking sand,
Sky threatens sea where our new frontier forms,
Sketched by ragged flights of gulls and terns,
Writing the winged unfathomable language
Of a future we must now learn to read.

CAROL V. DAVIS

Speaking in Tongues

In unfamiliar landscapes
Yiddish diminutives, terms of endearment,
drop my tongue, morsels, a little sweet, a little sour.

Then the curses begin their training: bulking up
on a diet of sarcasm and sneers, centuries of practice
honed to this art.

The Wyoming cowboys in the bar
stare at me in disbelief.
They're used to horses that whinny but this sounds
like something you'd attach to those decorated manes,
the kind no real cowboy would get near.

A geologist, also not from these parts, explains in a tone
reserved for restless third graders, just how to find a vein of coal.
Never mind the tops of mountains sheared off crew-cut style.
If he doesn't find it, someone else will.

In Virginia they asked if
I'd ever seen a real movie star. I've seen plenty:
without all that makeup, they're not so special.

Those cowboys really did tie bandanas around their necks;
you could tell they knew knotting from birth.
They didn't have to scuff their boots to show they meant business.

These curses didn't know where to go. The bar was full.
Every time one fiddler sat down, another jumped in.
Barely room to squeeze in between one slide of a bow and the next.
The windows fogged up; outside the snow thickened like insulation.
It was time to get serious: the curses hauled out
everything they had and let them have it.

NATHAN ALLING LONG

FICTION

Thrown

In the sense that there was nothing before it, all writing
is writing against the void. —Mark Strand

The seamless expanse of the white white snow had been enough to terrify him. No horse. No ice-blue shadow of hoof prints. No ephemeral outline of barn or tree etched on the horizon. No instinct of North, South, East, or West.

How long had he been knocked out? Where exactly was he when he had fallen? How long ago had Mosby run off? The snow swept past him in millions of tiny fragments. He looked again for a trace of anything, but saw only white, above and below. If gravity were to fail, there would even be no telling ground from sky.

His body was stiff from the fall, but the snow had cushioned him from breaking any bones. He yelled out for Mosby again, and after the horse did not appear, he did what he often did in infrequent encounters with terror; he thought of the mundane, listing what was certain. "This is snow," he whispered into the wind. "My feet are dry and my boots are on tight."

He knew enough not to panic—that was all. Once a steer had fallen on him, dead, and crushed his leg. He had waited five hours before being discovered, and another two before they could find enough help and chains to pull the animal off him. He had learned not to panic then, though both his legs had been numb and the cold mud of September had broken his body into shivers after the first hour.

But this situation was more serious. No one knew he was out here in the blizzard. And though he could stand and walk, he didn't know which way to turn.

Beneath this snow, he thought, *is my land*. He had lived and worked on this ranch for twelve years and knew well what lay beneath the surface of the ice. He thought of digging down to a patch of grass and dirt, to see if he could recognize the particular spot he was standing on. But even if he recognized it, which direction should he walk?

He had never been religious. It was dangerous to start now. Gods, from what he had noticed, were omnipotent, but also fickle. Especially gods of nature. They disliked late converts. The wind would just have to believe he had always revered it. He would have to hope, in silence, that it would offer the right direction home.

He began stepping cautiously forward, wary he could easily end up walking in circles. Was it better to run and be warmed, or be still and conserve energy? After all his years of winter, he couldn't say for sure. He searched for a gnarled tree, that boulder near the center of the upper plain. But even if something familiar had risen out of the surface of the snow into the edge of his vision, finding the barn or the house from there still seemed unlikely. How many steps would it take before the landmark would disappear again and his direction became uncertain? Two, or maybe three.

Then it happened, the black spots. They seemed both distant and near, and he blinked his eyes to make sure he was not simply imagining them. They weren't illusion, though; in fact, they were increasing—dark ashen flakes of snow, like static, falling from the sky and leaving patterns of black on the white ground.

He stopped thinking about direction. His mind struggled to understand what the black specks were. Perhaps a plane had exploded high above. Or a bomb—though wouldn't he have heard it, even through the roar of the wind? And why a bomb, way out here on the plains?

He could not help but think of other disasters, of that earthquake in San Francisco fifteen years ago, of Mount Saint Helen's, and of course, of the buildings falling in New York. And he thought of that story he had read in high school of the man building a fire in the wilderness, then realized how similar it was to the situation he was in. Had the character made it in that story? He didn't think he had.

The black snow landed on his shoulders and shoes, like tiny fingers leaving marks that would not melt. He felt he had to escape this blackness more than the cold itself. He began to walk faster and faster, until he was running. The frozen air cut his throat and lungs, though he had wrapped his scarf twice over his mouth. But no matter how far he ran, he always found himself in an identical blinding white space, with the black specks endlessly falling around him.

When he finally ran out of breath, he slowed to a walking pace, then stopped moving altogether. What was the point of going forward when it seemed to take you nowhere?

He stood silently then and listened. The wind picked up and the black and white snow flickered endlessly past his eyes. The seamless surface of the ground seemed to him then to be like the skin of a body. He had never been with anyone before, and he wondered, as he stood in the white silence, Why not? Why had he spent his years in barns grooming horses, in pastures mending fences, in endless fields searching, such as in this night, for lost cattle—and never discovered the landscape of another person's body? He couldn't say for sure.

Of course, there had been Mosby, his horse, whom he had known for almost ten years. His hand had memorized every muscle and bone of her body as he brushed her down each evening before feeding her. He had often pressed against her just to feel her heat enter his clothes. He had even slept beside her a few nights after she had been attacked by a coyote and could not stand. But now even she was gone—this bothered him more than anything. He stood silent against the wind, wondering what had happened to Mosby.

Gradually, he grew tired and knelt on the ground. His mind fell into long memories of riding through tall grass fields in summer, and after some un-known amount of time, he found himself numb, crawling across the snow, with the hypothermal hallucination that he was about to find the edge of the storm, lift it up, and crawl safely beneath it, as though it were an enormous blanket.

The cold bright snow had agitated Mosby, who, once freed from the weight of her owner, had run full force into the storm. Some instinct of direction, which had not been diminished by training, eventually led her home. After trying to wedge her way into her locked stall, she circled the barn, pressing against every door she found. Finally the tack room door, which was un-latched, swung open to the force of her head.

Inside there was light, and bales of hay, and—surprisingly—heat. A gasoline heater was left on to keep the saddle and tack supple and to keep the faucet used for filling the water buckets from freezing. Soon though, with the door half open, the room grew cold, and the thermostat re-ignited the heater with a *whoosh*.

The sound scared Mosby, and she stomped erratically around the small room. One front hoof caught the edge of the heater and knocked it over. The gasoline gurgled onto remnants of straw scattered on the floor (the shut-off valve, which had once been removed, had never been replaced). The fumes ignited and fire spread to the bales of hay stacked along the far wall. At first the quiet hush of the flames soothed Mosby. But then the flickering light frightened her, and she backed away, pressing her body against the door until it shut behind her. The room grew hot, and finally the heater itself exploded in a loud flash of white.

The particles of barn, horse, and hay—now cinders and ash—floated up into the cloud-white sky. They met the cold front that had brought in the storm, and it carried them that untold distance, back to the man lost in the white field of snow. In this way, she had returned to him.

MATT SCHUMACHER

Horse Heaven

What if all the wild horses went to heaven in Oregon
on this ridge named for their celestial ascent,
and shattered the grates
over the abandoned cinnabar mines,
galloping unscathed through the barbed wire
and no trespassing signs,
the missing beams of fabulously leaning cabins,
and their living and dead interbred,
transparent stallions grasping mist-breathed mares,
until life and death no longer mattered,
and dun-gray or red foals glowed like clouds
passing over the sun in the Ochoco Mountains,
and these lost descendants of Spanish mustangs
strode like conquistadors,
became famously unable to be tamed,
for no human could ever catch them,
they were so quicksilver fast
we could only glimpse their equine outlines
and they'd disappear at will,
long-maned, outracing
the ridiculous pickup trucks
of the bureau of land management,
their glossy shades fading
into suffocating dust.

KIRBY WRIGHT

Butchering Day

Sever my arthritic feet,
Toss them to coyotes
Hunting in packs

In the Mojave.
Fresh meat in pain
Is still fresh meat.

Let them taste
Poetry in my blood.
Watch them gnaw

Ankles, tendons, toes.
Hear them howl
When I tumble

Into their bellies
Under the blue moon
Of butchering day.

DAVID J. ROTHMAN

Tunnel of Love

Suddenly, in one quick, fluid move,
She stood up, stamped her foot, yelled "What an asshole!"
Swept the leather bag up off the table,
Slinging its long strap across her shoulder,
Grabbed the well-oiled, gleaming .38
Her Daddy left to her the day he died,
The one he'd used his whole time on the force
And which she'd contemplated where it lay
As hot, slow hours drifted by, and grabbed
One of the little boxes full of bullets
She'd dug out of the closet with the gun.

Ignoring even to stub out the spark
Of her bad, smoldering, umpteenth cigarette,
Which she now left half-balanced on the edge
Of an overstuffed, clay ashtray where its plume
Curled into summer, she walked to the car,
Pulled open the driver's door, threw gun and bullets
Across onto the passenger seat, sat down,
Hitched up her skirt a bit between her legs
So that it wouldn't interfere, and fumbling
For her keys and cursing, finding them
Buried in the bag with lipstick, combs,
Loose change, a small address book, lighters, gum,
More cigarettes, pens, Kleenex packets, matches,
Picking out the right key and then jamming
It down into the chrome ignition slot
With spastic rage, as if it were the car
That had offended her, paused for a second
Considering if what she planned to do
Was worth it, knowing thinking didn't matter

At this point, that the knots in her cold stomach
And at her temples spoke with the authority
Of gods brought back to life, now hungry, free,
And demanding to be fed immediately.

Without another thought she flipped the lights,
And punched the old Dodge Ram into reverse,
Making it describe a rocking circle
Back toward the rotting barn, then, after muscling
The stick up through geometry to first,
She freed the clutch and hit the gas too hard,
The way a drunk might kick a begging dog,
Which made the car skid toward the gate, then through
And out onto the pavement, where she threw
An underdog's hard left, palming the wheel
While shifting sloppily to second gear,
Fishtailing back into the late-night lane,
A darkened ribbon pointing down at town
Like one of Cupid's perfect, poisoned arrows.

"You son of a bitch," she said, and meant it too,
As soon as he had opened the peeling door,
Wearing a grungy, sleeveless undershirt,
A beer in his left hand, her name's one syllable
Dying on his lips as he found himself
Forgetting what commercial he'd been watching,
Because he now stood staring down the fat
Dark barrel of a .38 held steadily
By the two trained hands of a sergeant's only daughter,
Whom he knew knew her shooting as he'd seen her
Blow skeet to hopeless pieces in one shot
As fast as she could yell the short word "Pull!",
Sometimes ten times in a row, and then just laugh,
The ground around her littered with spent shells,
The beautiful blond ringlets of her hair
Cascading around the knowing smile she'd send
His way as she announced, with a laugh, "Your turn."

* * *

"You son of a bitch," she said, "do you think you
Can sleep with her, and in a town this small,
When she's my best friend and my family
Knows everybody, and I won't find out,
Or do you think I'm stupid, like your buddies,
Or I love your damned lies so much I'd blink
If you joined hips with my pretty, flirting aunt,
Or that I wouldn't think, because she's married
And has two kids, a home, a jealous husband,
That she could possibly allow you in,
As if that hasn't held her back before,
As if she doesn't have a history,
That I, despite our friendship, know full well,
Or did you think you'd get away with it,
Like every hot-shot arrogant bullshit artist
Who fantasizes that because his hands
Can master all the bent and broken engines
In this small, beastly burg, and as he works
In sponsored pits and confidently struts
With carburetor, line, and pump know-how,
That he can jerk around a breathing person
As if she were just one more greased machine,
When fact is that I am a living woman,
Who though to you is nothing but a valve
Through which to stroke your desperate little ego,
Is, let me tell you, you two-timing mouse,
You slippery dishonest narcissistic
Emotional Quasimodo sewer-snake,
You loathsome, ethical-castrato rat,
Angry, and furthermore let me tell you
That this time you have made a real mistake,
Have burned the wrong 'babe,' as I bet you call them
When post-race bar-side with the other boys

You toast yourselves and feebly try to converse,
A pack of horny troglodytes with beer,
And mister, let me tell you something else
Before I blow your brains all over the bookshelf,
Which don't think I won't do or don't know how,
You slept with me and whispered your sweet sweetnesses
All up and down my soft neck's downiest hairs,
And I believed your songs about a house,
With friendly dog and renovated plumbing
That you said you would get down on your knees
And fix the way I bet you think you can
Fix this fine mess although this time it's over
And the disposal's just about to break,
Oh yes, I held those words of yours as true
As pleasures that we made, and that's the lie
That's going to put a bullet in your gullet,
For if I hadn't bought that stream of honey,
If you'd been lucky enough to bore me sleepy,
I wouldn't give a jolly good God damn
Whose heart you diddled, but you were too good,
Too lovely and delicious, too coordinated,
You pig hyena dog worm fly toad louse
Sloth vulture termite virus parasitic
No-good lily-livered feckless scorpion
Stone cold philandering peabrained cheapskate lowlife
Heartless coward malicious sybaritic
Byronesque Don Juan Lothario
Casanova Quisling Benedict Arnold
Brutus Judas Cassius Lucifer
Burgess Blunt MacLean Hiss Rosenberg
And Pollard-like deserting treacherous
Slimeball greasehair mechanic redneck dirtbag,
That may have been your first transgression but
It's also going to be your last sweet apple,"
And stamped her foot and by mistake squeezed off

A round that whistled over his left shoulder,
Traversed the little entryway, shot through
The living room where he'd been watching television,
Killing, in this case, only a sitcom
As it ripped directly through the box,
Which shattered, fizzled, cracked, and spat some smoke
While the bullet eagerly continued through
The kitchen door, passed over the small table
He'd bought not long ago at a tag sale,
And whose chipped surface was of cheap Formica
Inlaid with dull, abstract geometry,
Sort of like a lot of modern poems,
And finally punched a perfectly round hole
In a kitchen window screen and headed out
Over the apartment building's poor excuse
For lawn, the sidewalk, curb, then Old Town Highway,
Through a small patch of woods, across the lake,
Its dark waves glinting in the lonely starlight,
And then, on the other shore, the county line.

The friendly dog to which she had referred,
A chocolate lab whose name, of course, was Butch,
And which had stood, head cocked, as she went on,
Tail tentatively wagging, now realized
Just what was happening, and dived for safety,
Crawling underneath the dusty couch,
Not, it should be pointed out, a first.

"Uh, hi," he said, holding as cavalierly
As perhaps only an almost dead man can,
His beer, concentrating on not moving,
And trying to sweat as little as he could,
"Hi darling," and then, after a little pause,
In which he understood he was alive,
And that the bullet hadn't danced with him,
Which meant he might still save his sorry skin,

For she was waiting, almost as surprised
As he was by her finger, for the moment,
For something else to happen, unclear what,
But something from his lips before she did
With more intent and better aim the thing
She had just almost done before she wanted,
And so thin threads of possible sympathy
Still dangled him above the great abyss
To which he had no doubt she just might send him,
And even less that in some sense he did
Unquestionably deserve to take the trip,
"Lover, lover," he then said, "I'm sorry,"
And he paused, took one, long, slow sip of Bud,
In which he could not help imagining
What it might be like to see a tongue
Of flame and powder laser at his chest
Or head, the last thing he would ever see,
Before some part, or rather, he imagined,
Many parts, considering the caliber
Of bore that he was contemplating now
So closely that it almost made him cross-eyed,
Of him were violently dispersed in agony.

All for twenty minutes of desire.

He calmly looked her in the eye, and slowly said,
With every cunning grace, and eggshell care:
"This rage to kill, its tragic worth, makes sense,
As real as my own shame, which has been gnawing
At me with nightmares, and if I still could
I would rebuild your dream, apologize,
And still work hammering my words back up
With nailed contrition, but I see the time
For framing new love's architecture's passed,
So I won't even start to honey out
These last few moments with the lies that lie

So sweetly beckoning erotic traitors
Out of some ancient, yellow courtesy book,
Because it's clear no engine in your soul
Could honor this false face now knowing that
I have indeed delighted in the charms,
However mediocre, of that slut,
Your aunt and untrue friend, disloyal Mary,
Whose eyes often undressed this very shirt
As we all talked penultimate lap tactics
Over beers at Willy's after victory,
And who, in desperation with unhappiness
At life, in love, at growing older now
And looking at her beauty growing dry,
Decided I, the man who loved her niece,
The younger friend in whom she sees herself
A decade gone, was the man to hold, to press
And clutch a nakedness against her anger,
Against the empty loneliness she hears
Approaching as you come into your own,
Because she hates the way our easy bodies
Soar into what we are, above the sour
And twisted marriage where she's bound her hands,
Well, no, I can't apologize for that,
What's done is done, and done for good or ill,
But what still works against my memory
Is the taste of my own inability,
The ignorance in each memory of time's
Hard-pressed affection running through our fingers
Like sand or water as we made time wait
The small details of any given day,
And then the sweating fire of every taste
We've ever had of one another's love
Such as the first time, here, on my thin bed,
Which bent, then one day broke in rapt surprise,
Then on the rug, against the sink, your place,

In the barn and on the roof that endless day
In sweatiest July when the sun seemed stuck
In our sky like a witness to our energy."

He slowly took a single sip of beer.

"But let me tell you this one time before
You squirt fool's lead somewhere into my failures,
And by opposing, end them: I, in treachery,
Blind and blinded simply by a body,
Discovered as I might have in no way
Outside that single flashpoint of unconsciousness,
What spark has come to move my every limb,
Which was your single name on my sad tongue,
As lacking love or even its strange ghost
I kissed and wrestled with that sultry wench,
Your aunt and so-called friend, the nasty Mary,
Whose disappointing body only served
As the vehicle for this slow recognition,
That my ripe love for who you are grows up—
Although it's true perhaps that I have not—
And canopies around my life like palms,
Yet roots so deeply, like an oak, that I
Can't turn against it if I choose to turn,
For I am turned tree too by the truth of one
Unthought and coward moment of deception,
In which I now see I made a mistake,
And that no name but yours with its real contours
And human imperfections can outline
The lonely curve of sleep, that infidelity
Was error, and not just because wrong, right?
But more, because untrue, untrue to life,
That, darling," he sighed, "this is bigger than
The both of us."

                    He looked at her and hoped.

She paused, and then "Go screw yourself" she snarled,
But his left, sweaty hand already held
Her two, and swayed them slightly, and the bullet
Went ten degrees awry and merely sliced
One of his denim belt loops before shattering
The dog dish and then burying itself
Deep in a beam beneath the cheap pine floor
Which had been painted many times before
One owner lay down bad linoleum.

The dog, whose tail was visible, yelped once.

Or would you have it otherwise? Would you?
Would you prefer to see the moment end,
This beautiful, untrue young man blown down,
Eyes rolling back, blood everywhere, the gun
Thrown down in horror as she holds his head,
And now to see him twitching uncontrollably,
And he once whimpers "I'm so cold," then dies?

Remember, they are nothing, just like you,
It's all a nothing, and a man is nothing,
It's nothing and a man is nothing too,
And yet they are so lovely, like two leaves
On a gigantic oak tree in the spring,
Yes sweet mortality, ripe, rich, and cunning
Beneath the sky and sun that will die blind
And blacken to the heart, good, great oasis
In the desert of eternity, O tree,
I marvel at your darling bark and press
My arms and chest and lips against your own,
To make my prayer: make me a vicious horsefly
With a sting like fire and set me in that room.

He had forgotten just how strong she was,
Almost like a goddess and well-trained
By her old man, the cop, who'd always said

"You never know, this stuff might come in handy,"
And so he was surprised when, though off balance,
She took a step back, wrenched the pistol free,
And kicked him in the stomach with her instep
As if he were a human soccer ball,
Connecting like a goalie and doubling him over,
Which made him toss his beer against the wall,
And lining up her aim again, though now
The barrel pointed down into his face,
In which his eyes were swimming like poor rats
Who cannot leave the ship they know is sinking.

This is the point at which the vicious horsefly,
Which does not give a damn about a thing
Except sweet blood, connected with a spot
One inch above the collar of her shirt,
And bit her, bit the goddess like a nail,
Which made her yell and jerk and smack a hand
On the unlucky bug, who squished and died
As her tense trigger finger squeezed again,
Sending bullet number three away
Into the door of the refrigerator,
And through a week-old carton of sour milk
Which started glopping down onto a sandwich
As the bullet pounded wet into the wall
And he tripped forward, groaning, knocking her
And him together down onto the floor,
The wild gray gun gone clattering across it
Into the bubbling puddle of warm beer
As she beat on his back with balled-up fists
And tried to lift him off, too much for her,
Despite the anger and the dark-eyed passion.

It was the smell more than the fact, the smell
Which passion metamorphosed out of rage
Back down into the mortal realm of love,

His smell as he lay groaning on her chest
Which suddenly unhinged her anger's danger,
And slyly opened her down back to what
She might have done, had almost done, almost,
His smell, a smell of sweat and beer and him,
Disgusting, irreplaceable, like gravity,
And now, like death, completely irresistible,
Which opened up her hands upon his back
From fists to palms that held him as she wept.
"This chick is nuts," he whispered to himself,
But fortunately she had kicked his gut
So hard he didn't have the wind to say
Such a stupid, self-destructive thing,
But only wheezed as she brought her sweet lips
Against his own and held him there until
He nearly suffocated, though by now
He'd realized he was alive and she
Was utterly alive and holding him
On top of her, and her smell struck his brain
In one Promethean inhalation of fire,
Reviving him, reviving every part
Into the true, ongoing, lonesome sound
Of love, lovemaking, warmth, and possibility.

"I thought three bullets would be enough," she said,
Turning her head away to get a breath
As he was fumbling crazy with his zipper,
Whose teeth he then ripped out exasperated,
While kissing her again, locked in a hammer hold
Of love and sweat which tumbled them back down,
As she was on her back, he on his knees,
Hands occupied, into the little table
Which held the telephone that now went flying,
Although it didn't matter, as they landed
Tangled in the cord, which ripped it out
Of the square, brown plastic socket modifier,
Which sounded like a champagne cork gone south.

* * *

Let us go then, as the rest is obvious,
The ecstasy of tigers, strong, alive,
Alive as ever any sweet thing was,
Unable and uncaring to outsing
Time's jangling chains, to stop their mad pursuit
Of life, which they have rolled into themselves
And hurled wherever they can make it go,
Behind, before, above, between, below,
Bursting electric out of the dark wood
Of lies and rage into the ordinary,
The ordinary world where they most certainly
Will treat each other right, or maybe not,
As outside in the cold, dark distant night
The great oak reaches up into the stars
That are themselves just other rustling leaves
Which drift across vast emptiness, whose voids
Are also leaves, all whispering the secret
Of immortality and tenderness,
Inhuman hawk flight and one sweet caress
Against the endless peaceful restlessness
Within which, in some dim, forgotten town
A dog has stuck his head out from beneath
A dusty couch to watch with mild bewilderment
His master and the woman whom he loves
Recreating the entire universe.

THE LEY OF THE LAND

GEORGE DAVID CLARK

Gilapause

Tonight, like knots of pillow
lava in vanilla sand, the Gila

monsters galvanize and spill
through vents to stormlight.

They blink chill, yellow eyes,
their burrows seething

until gravity unclenches
and they crawl the gray

Sonoran craterscape
like spiders on a ceiling.

Loosed and sprawled, I clutch
a buckhorn cholla by its neck

while bits of dust and gravel
billow out toward the satellites.

Saguaro chandeliers hang
in the un-electric haze.

Their sallow quill-lights flicker.
If my upper lip beads warm

tequila, stud-skinned Gilas flex
their fangs. My fingernails

can only follow the little threads
of sandfall back so far

into the salty reaches
of the dry arroyo,

and beneath my dangling
a lightning-lipped darkness
swallows, swallows, swallows.

WENDY VIDELOCK

Coyote

Coyote,
we hardly know you,
which
like coyote nose,
is the point

of all coyote
glory and holy
revelation.

In our backyard
coyote ignores
the steady, pale
climb of the moon.

Old hat.
Done that.

Instead he picks his fights
with Thor,

the god who dares
descend
and wrangle back,

bringing coyote,
minor god,
ferocious little

deity,
a scrap
of coyote dignity

and several existential
yaps
and moans
closer to home.

TERESA MILBRODT

Shopping with Grandpa

Grandpa became a cowboy after the war, or at least he always wore the hat when he left his apartment, including when I took him on Saturday afternoon trips to the grocery store. He tried to corrupt me with junk food, especially Pop-Tarts, the ones with brown sugar or chocolate filling that I couldn't pretend were even a little healthy. He knew I'd bring them over to his apartment for us to eat while flipping through horse tack catalogs. Even though he's passed away, Grandpa is still tempting me to buy Pop-Tarts as I purchase organic apples, carrots, and bell peppers.

You need to treat yourself sometimes, he says. *You're too thin, like your grandma. Men like women with meat on their bones.* I swear I can smell his cigarette smoke in the produce section when there isn't anyone else around. I sniff my sleeve to see if I still carry the odor of his apartment, but no, I just smell like detergent. In the cereal aisle I buy blueberry Pop-Tarts.

They're not even frosted, grumps Grandpa.

No, they're not, I think back to him, but I know I'll come back before checking out and buy pink-frosted strawberry ones. *You trained me too well.*

That's my girl, says Grandpa.

I took him shopping when he could no longer drive, after I'd taken away his car keys following the third parking lot fender-bender. He still shops with me on Saturdays, bitching and laughing and telling stories and convincing me to buy sugary cereal. Sometimes we finished off a box in an afternoon while he told me about the latest horse he was going to buy, right after he got his next Social Security check.

All that cereal wasn't too bad for us, he reminds me. *We could have been eating worse.*

I don't know if this is a haunting or if because I spent so much time with him, my brain can't rid itself of our call-and-response. I was the first grandchild, and maybe this is part of my inheritance. Somehow Grandpa even managed to haunt me when he was alive.

The first time it happened I was in Germany, traveling around mainland Europe before I spent a semester studying abroad in England. I was curious to experience the cold damp of the British Isles after growing up in arid Colorado. It was the late nineties, a decade after the Berlin Wall came down. It was being sold in pieces in outdoor markets, a symbol of communism turned into a symbol of capitalism. Grandpa said he would be thinking about me, but I didn't realize his voice would trail me to the Tiergarten and Checkpoint Charlie museum, whispering stories from the war.

When I was traveling with the Third Army, we found office buildings in Germany that had been abandoned. That's when I found the identification card from a German soldier. Even now I wonder if that young man survived. He looked my age. In the smoky living room of my brain, Grandpa lit another cigarette and teared quietly, pulling on the brim of his cowboy hat like he did when he wanted to hide a memory. I smelled the smoke from his hand-rolled cigarette as I sat in a German cafe, ordered an apple pastry, and tried to dry his tears from my mind. Grandpa said real cowboys always rolled their own cigarettes.

I was the first person in our family to travel to Germany since WWII, when my grandpa was drafted but petitioned not to fight. He drove through the war, transporting captains and chaplains in a jeep. Since he was from the west he was used to traveling long distances on rough roads, but he hated guns. Like the rest of the boys he came home a hero, but heroes were not supposed to cry or have nightmares, especially in stoic cowboy cattle country. Heroes were allowed to smoke, which he'd never done before the war, and which

Grandma didn't let him do in the house because she said it was a smelly habit.

"I had to smoke on the porch, or in the garage with the paint cans and oil rags," he told me. "Don't know why I didn't blow us all to kingdom come."

My grandparents had three kids, two daughters and a son four years apart. Grandpa got a job with the school district as a bus mechanic, since he was good at doctoring engines. He'd brought a box of stuff home from the war, souvenirs and pictures, but he wouldn't let anyone look at it. At meals he was quiet, ate and nodded his thanks to Grandma and went outside to smoke. Their house was on the edge of town, so he could sit on the porch with his cowboy hat, stare at the mesas, and look stoic.

"What happened to you?" Grandma asked him every night as she stood in front of the porch door. Grandpa didn't have an answer, just rolled another cigarette.

"Sometimes he was quiet and almost sweet," my mom remembers. "Other times he'd snap and stomp away from the table if the soup was too cold or one of us kids had done badly on a test. He'd yell at us about not valuing our education. It was like Dr. Jekyll and Mr. Dad. Or maybe Wyatt Earp and Butch Cassidy."

"The worst thing I ever did was hit your grandma," Grandpa told me. "I got mad at her for some fool thing. Maybe the kitchen floor wasn't clean enough. She asked me who the hell I'd become. The question got me so angry that—" He shook his head. "I left to get a couple burritos in town, and when I got back, my bag was packed and on the porch."

Mom was in college, and my aunt and uncle were almost out of high school. Grandpa moved into a smelly apartment and stayed there for the rest of his life, opening the window to air the place out when Mom came to visit. After I was born, he wanted to see me all the time. I was a second chance, an opportunity for him to watch a kid grow up. At least that's what Mom thinks.

"Dad was a provider," she told me. "Not a dad. When you came along, he was ready to be a grandpa."

If she was jealous of the way he bought a cowgirl outfit with a pink hat for me, and took me on the Ferris wheel and carousel at the county fair, she never let on. Grandpa wanted to take me on the pony rides, but I was scared of horses. When I was in elementary school, he kept promising to pay for riding lessons I didn't want. I loved my cowgirl outfit with the fringe, but I wasn't going to get on a horse no matter what Grandpa dreamed. He might have wanted an excuse to hang out around the stables and meet real cowboys so he could perfect his fantasies, but I think he did a good job on his own.

My aunt and uncle didn't bring my cousins to see him, but Grandma invited him to Thanksgiving and Christmas though they stayed in different rooms. Grandpa was quiet and smiling, but then some small thing would set him off, usually noisy kids or a political remark from one of my uncles about the latest conflict in the Middle East.

"Blast it, can't a man get some peace?" he'd yell before stomping to the porch for a cigarette. The outbursts scared my cousins, but I was used to them. That was Grandpa needing solitude. I'd wander out to find him and bring cookies or a piece of pie for each of us. Many of our holiday desserts were consumed in the freezing cold on my grandma's front porch.

"Come spring I'll finally buy my horse," he said, kissing the top of my head.

I nodded because even when I was eight years old, I knew it was his job to tell that story and my job to agree with it. Grandpa was always driving across the state to some ranch to look at horses. He never went riding as far as I know, but made good friends with a few ranchers who were sympathetic to the cowboy dreams of a veteran-turned-school-bus-mechanic. Sometimes they asked him to work on their tractors, probably to give him an excuse to visit and fantasize.

Grandpa makes me pause in the frozen foods aisle, looking at the fried chicken and mashed potato meals that were his favorite.

They're too high in sodium, I think, walking past to buy skinned chicken breast.

You're no fun, says Grandpa, but even in my head he's smiling.

I was the only person in the family who stopped by his apartment, usually with cookies. I smelled like smoke after every visit. Mom couldn't stand the stench but never said anything about it. She sympathized with him, even if she didn't want to go over and hang out and look through tack catalogs.

In college when I was debating between journalism and psychology as a major, I took enough psych classes to think I knew what I was doing in diagnosing Grandpa's multiple conditions that made him resort to cowboy wanna-beism. I recited all the clinical names for what he probably had because of the war—survivor's guilt, post-traumatic stress syndrome, flashbacks—but Grandpa waved his hand to brush my words away.

"It doesn't matter," he said. "I've felt like shit on and off for fifty years, and I don't think that'll change any time soon." He tugged on the brim of his cowboy hat. "Last weekend I was back to that ranch north of Durango. There's a horse I might buy, a paint with nice markings. I might drive down again soon and check him out again."

And breeze through the beautiful middle-of-nowhere in his pickup with over two hundred thousand miles on it. Somehow he kept coaxing life out of that engine year after year because he loved the truck. The truck probably loved him. Grandpa had named it Trigger.

"I don't know how cowboys covered all that ground when they were still grazing cattle on the open range and doing the cattle drives to Denver," I told him as we ate Pop-Tarts. I wasn't sure if Grandpa would have enjoyed that lifestyle, but I wasn't going to say that directly.

"They had a rough life," he said with a nod, "but things were more focused back then. Folks didn't live as long, but they had real purpose. You wake up, make breakfast, tend to your horses and cows until it's too dark to see, make dinner, go to sleep, and try not to be bitten by a rattler or get cholera or yellow fever." It was the rugged, solitary, innocent world he envied, even if he wouldn't have reached his fiftieth birthday.

"Why live to be ninety if you're not having fun?" he asked me.

"Are you not having fun?" I asked.

Grandpa unwrapped another Pop-Tart. "I have fun when you come over," he said. "And when I'm in the truck. Or looking at them horses. That's fun."

He must have been haunted by things I couldn't see, war movies that played over and over on the too-vivid screen in his mind. He tried to replace those films with Westerns they showed on Saturday afternoons, chain-smoking in his apartment as he watched John Wayne stoically save the day, since that was the way John Wayne did everything.

* * *

Twice I went on drives with my grandpa to look at horses, but I don't remember the visits to those ranches as much as I remember the look in his eyes as we walked around, how he gazed at the mountains and mesas with a concerned squint, like he was seeing the ghosts of soldiers and cowboys working alongside ranch hands. Both times on the way home, he talked about the war.

"There was so much destruction," he told me. "In France. In Germany. So many young people dying. So many children going hungry."

He lit another cigarette and wiped his eyes with the side of his hand.

"Maybe you should talk to someone," I said. "A professional."

"I don't want to tell this shit to a shrink," he said. "It's too personal. And it's family history, things you should hear."

He looked from side to side like the ghosts of cowboys were still with us, riding along the shoulder and keeping pace with our truck, but they were concerned with important things like keeping their herds alive. After visiting those ranches with Grandpa, I decided against the psychology major. I didn't know what to do with his wandering stories or the ghosts he saw and wouldn't tell me about. When he died I figured he'd join them, the specters of ranchers and cowboys and soldiers meandering around mountains, but instead he comes with me to the grocery.

I smell cigarette smoke in the pasta aisle and listen to Grandpa mumbling as I decide between seashells or rotini. Our culture doesn't know how to deal with seeing dead people, though we do it all the time. When people admit to it we call them crazy.

Could you please be quiet for a little bit? I ask Grandpa.

I should have lost my left foot, he says. *Right after I got over there. I would have been out of the war much earlier. Just a little sacrifice, but people would have respected it. They would have seen I was injured. Maybe it would have been okay to cry. But then I couldn't have ridden a horse.*

You never rode a horse anyway, I think to him.

That's beside the point, he says. I don't know if it's good or bad that I know he's right.

His voice in my head cracks and fades. I take a deep breath and choose rotini.

Because I'm a reporter I think a lot about stories–telling them, being haunted by them, trying to replace one story with another. My grandpa didn't like his story, which explains why he kept writing a new one over top, choosing the biggest one he could find and making revisions accordingly while he tugged on the brim of his hat.

My cousins all thought he was a crazy old man, and even my aunt and uncle didn't want to deal with him much, but it was understandable. Wounded people aren't always nice people. I tried explaining that to my cousins, how the angry Grandpa wasn't the real Grandpa, but trauma inhabiting his body like an evil spirit. Dreaming of cowboys was a kind of exorcism, letting him drift into a hard and simple world of chaps and spurs and quietude.

My cousins nodded and continued to avoid him at holiday gatherings, but just as the world withdrew from Grandpa, Grandpa withdrew from the world. This is easy in the west, and maybe even a tradition since we have so much space. Grandpa only asked that I take him grocery shopping and bring him a copy of the daily paper so he could read my latest articles, which he cut out and put in a folder he planned to turn into a scrapbook.

"I'd ask you to write my autobiography," he told me, "but it's not done yet. I haven't gotten to the important parts. Like when Mitch and I go camping in the desert."

Mitch was Grandpa's age, a guy who'd moved into an apartment down the hall. His dad had bred horses when Mitch was younger, and he had a bad back from a riding accident years ago, but Mitch said he was going to start riding again and take Grandpa with him so he'd have a student.

"Best way to remember how to do something is to teach someone else," Mitch said. He loved Grandpa's hand-rolled cigarettes, so many times I found them sitting around his kitchen table, all the windows open even in the middle of January. They were lost in a cloud of smoke, hunched over coffee cups and cheap oatmeal cookies, looking at some horse magazine or riding gear catalog and making plans.

"Damn this country," Grandpa said. "A man works his whole life to earn an honest dollar, then in his old age he doesn't have the money to buy a good horse."

"My nephew's got a few horses that are broke," Mitch said. "We could try them out."

"A man needs his own horse," Grandpa said, adding more sugar to his coffee. "It's not right to deny him that."

"I s'pose not," said Mitch. He never pressed Grandpa on the issue, so I didn't know if he had cowboy dreams or cowboy nightmares. Maybe a little of both. Mitch and Grandpa listened with wide eyes when I told them about the rodeo riders I interviewed, young men who wore helmets when they mounted steers and bucking broncos, trying to hold on and not break their necks. After I wrote an article about the twenty-three-year-old bronco buster who'd become paralyzed from the waist down, Grandpa decided I should never get on the back of a horse, but it was still okay for him.

"I'm old," he said. "I can afford to be stupid."

When I put my strawberry-frosted Pop Tarts on the conveyor belt at the checkout, I think, *Now that you're gone I guess I should take some riding lessons. It would give me more to write about.*

Young lady, if you break your back falling off of a horse, I will never speak to you again.

Is that a threat or an incentive? I think, but we were always sarcastic like that.

At least you got the right kind of Pop-Tarts, he says.

You trained me too well, I think, missing the extra weight of his chicken dinners and even the canned peas in my plastic shopping bags, but it's those little things that make us choke up as we carry our organic carrots to the car and sniff the air, hoping for the little whiff of cigarette smoke that means we're not alone.

GEORGE DAVID CLARK

Cold Night Near Cody

What falls across the headstones makes no sound
unless you count the hush of moon on snow.
It's a cold night to be dead and in the ground.

We bought this graveside acreage out of town
to hear the music an evening's prose,
but what falls across the headstones makes no sound.

Our little farmhouse sinks under the pounds
of powder till the lot almost plateaus.
It's a cold night to be dead and in the ground.

Colossal stacks of cymbals, firs are crowned
and crisped; the ditch a flute of ice, and even so,
what falls across the headstones makes no sound.

Abashed, harassed by stillness, silence-gowned,
we slide our robes off underneath the bedclothes.
It's a cold night to be dead and in the ground

and waiting for a trumpet to shout down
a hallelujah. Here, no angel blows.
What falls across the headstones makes no sound.
It's a cold night to be dead and in the ground.

WENDY VIDELOCK

No Tobacco

No tobacco,
no meat,
no weed,
no soda—
everybody
goin' yoga.

FICTION

Genghis' Knoll

How'd she turn the engine over? Set aside the gun? She couldn't have. In her retreated mind, in this present, all she recalls is her head aching a starry rhythm. Remembers she flattened the gas pedal, peeled away. Burning oil, clumps of mudded rock pinging the truck's chassis. Windows down. Wind clearing her eyes. Wind fanning tears across her dry cheeks as washboards rattled her chest, jangling like her heart might unfix, fall loose—wanting madly to let it, ditch the worthless organ in the dust because up to then she didn't know she had it.

Corny. Sound corny to you? Well, up yours. Were you back in Nebraska, back where she scrapped it, there with her old man standing limp in their clapboard kitchen? You there with your quaky old lady, Papa's neck skin fresh under her fingernails?

Ah, so that's why she—

No, not that easy. If she could now, she'd admit her actions were destructive, OK, and she knew it, yes, but . . . But she *never* wished to die. Whatever it was coming up and out of her, that's what she needed to end—fishtailing hard dirt corners, pebbled-ruts jolting, throwing earth from the front wheels into the cockeyed beams of her truck. Head clouded like the windshield, clouded so she couldn't tell the difference between here and there, now and then, before and after. Isn't there hard blue night beyond those headlights? She cocks the gun's hammer. Howls growing louder—coyotes on her heels, hunting, and with Genghis gone they've got nothing to stop them.

Jesus, does she still owe the beasts? Can't take her eyes off the road, can't unlock her left fist from the wheel, fingers of her right from the .38. Can't turn her head to see though she knows the passenger seat's empty, and something, that Other in her, *it* lifts the gun. Easy-slip barrel and damp, damp trigger. Softness of the roof of the mouth. Metal tapping, tapping. Like cattle-guard against tooth enamel. And the nurses leave as they always do. Zooming home. Her knee jerks. Feels her skeleton depress the gas pedal, feels the gas pedal depress time, feels time depress itself, rolling over onto history.

Every night the nurses zoom home. Zoom east because west are the mountains, the finish. Zooming with their voices high and light, fingernails clean. After they wheel her away from the windowsill. After they've stretched her— *No, only facedown, might choke on mucus, vomit*—on the thin mattress. Draped out, rigid again. And again she hits the cattle-guard going sixty plus.

No lollygagging, not really. Drove directly for the spot, Genghis' head drooped out the passenger window of her yellow Ford Courier. And she didn't speed, but she didn't take the longest route either. Simply getting there meant meandering. Northwest on Castle Height's red dirt roads and then due west through brown lawns and pastures giving way to scrub, to drooling breccia cliffs. How she would say if she could, without self-reproach, without exaggeration (and she does, though only she can feel the words), that the sky was literally miraculous that evening. When she returns to the moment, withered arms leaned hopelessly against this flaking paint, staring out at the rough gray lick of encroaching Wyoming horizon, the minutia of her existence under this cloud that never ebbs—those lyrics, that refrain, turn and turn behind her shattered eardrums: *Seen it rain and fire in the sky.*

Seen it. Rain and fire.
    Seen it. Timeless Idaho dusk, red-rimmed pastel paper clipped out, pasted on a blue screen. Of course, way back then the only John Denver song she could name was "Thank God I'm a Country Boy," and at eighteen she wouldn't have admitted knowing it, not for her life. *Country boy?* Hell, she and the old lady holed-up in a modular HUD duplex for fuck's fast sake. Mom's job

with City Parks weeding the fishing ponds in summer, driving that limp-shit Zamboni all winter. Country boy—she owned two flannel shirts and one pair of nasty Lees, so why give other girls that sort of ammunition? Why? Even though they'd instigate, she'd be the one to pay—

If only a cheek to bite, not this bubbled pink scar tissue.

On the northwest edge of their subdivision, the Ohio Canyon BLM gate. She ground her little truck to a halt. Jumping out, engine running, unlatched the chain. Swung it open with a metal groan, then back in the truck. Rattling over the cattle guard, and even though you're supposed to she didn't close it behind.

Continuing. Plugging into the hide-tan hills, mile by creeping mile. By then Genghis was flat drained, lugging his massive towhead in from the window, shifting his hips and falling over to rest his cheek on her thigh.

Snapshot: last sunbeams level into the cab, illuminating dashboard dust wisps, fur dancing, sinking, a fiery dry plankton. She rubs Genghis' neck tendons, scratches lightly his nape. Yesterday, they went to Eddie's for a hair-cut and the spikiness tickles her fingers. She tries laughing, even then, *even now*, making a sound meaning life's lighthearted especially at its close. Born in purple snot, die in it.

That's the second snapshot: tries to laugh away the blood-mucus gunk of the brain, runs her tongue behind her bottom lip saying, "Fuck it."

Sighs. "Fuck it, time to be men."

Genghis looked all runt and she picked him out that way. Smallest in the light blue nursery, skin and long bones. Like a challenge, it was. Told her mom she planned to get him big as Bunyan, and as soon as they got home she made Genghis a bed in the garage. Got right to feeding him extra from her chores money. Worked, too. He filled out in a matter of months, her mom saying, "Oh, he responds to you! He doesn't respond to me like that, nope, no way. Only you, like ESP. Now that's love, goddamn it, not obligation, not marriage to an idiot who can't get it up."

Without her mom saying so, she already knew all this. Genghis wasn't the submissive sort, either. Acted out of their collective interests—you could see it in his huge, gooey eyes—and by the time they got to Idaho he was the largest Dr. Denis ever heard of. Also the doc couldn't believe that at his mass Genghis was a Born, not an Accident. But her mom showed Genghis' papers, Dr. Denis going, "Holy smokes, that good!" and nodding at the signatures, fingering the gold seal. "It's official. His sire was a hefty one, too, looks like, and it's all muscle, so I'm not worried about him."

The dad's name was Steve, Genghis' mom Melinda. But she'd never met Genghis parents because they got Genghis from the Nebraska Rescue the day after her mom told her old man to go live in a hotel room and not off their savings. The rescue files had all of Genghis' papers, according to their documentation his parents decided not to keep him (and obviously not have him terminated) because, the files said, both were unemployed.

But the woman at the rescue told it differently. In a great hush she said Steve wasn't unemployed, but bucket-kicked, and her mom blurted, "*Dead?*"

"As your doorbell." The woman going on to explain this was why Melinda abandoned Junior—Genghis' birth name, for supposedly the fellas on Steve's softball team made a game of taunting him about his soul-less sperm, and, well, he snapped. "Guy started swinging his bat on the bench," the rescue woman whispered, "and—oh, tell me this doesn't define irony—gave two of the fellas brain damage before the other guys could jump him and, you know . . . ."

"No," she said, looking up from the floor, up at the two whispering women, "what?"

"Nothing," her mom snapped. "We get the picture."

In the car, taking Genghis home. Her old lady saying it was absolutely the worst thing she'd ever heard, all of it—Genghis' parents, the rescue worker, no couth, adults acting like animals, like children, everyone letting their imaginations run wild.

The girl's mouth opened. *Excuse me?* She almost said something . . . said. What, though? Something about Papa? There was connection, perfect synonyms, most of a syllogism but she missed it by a hair. Next thing she knew they were moving to Idaho.

* * *

North of Boise. That's when the headaches began. Or maybe they'd been there all along but that's when she started to register them? Like this one here, this one five miles up Ohio Canyon Road where the tire ruts grow faint and the wilderness closes in. She pulled her truck into the turn-around at the mouth of the wash. This was where she took her girlfriends, too. Every time, borrowing her mom's Plymouth wagon she'd convert the back into a bed with an egg-crate mattress, five blankets, couple pillows. Out in that nowhere then, in the cramped cold of the car, swimming in blackness and just the sound of saliva moving, she'd undress them until they were facedown and she'd say, "Ask me to fuck you with something random."

Hell, she wasn't a lesbo—this doesn't mean she was a lesbo.

"With . . . with what?"

"Do it. Ask me."

Sometimes they'd say it. But other times she'd just listen to their breath abbreviate, listen to the singing coyotes racing across the hard ground to encircle the car.

"It's a game."

"Those aren't wolves are they?"

"You know perfectly well what they are."

—except, why? Why'd they do it? Why'd they go out there with her, the wiry girl with one pair of jeans and two flannel shirts? Why was she the great murky rumor for forty percent of the girls in her puny high school? Because she did the things the guys didn't? Could it be that simple? All of it just the filling of negative space? That she did the things males and females, whether male *or* female, aren't supposed to do until much later in life?

Yes? Maybe? What's the opposite of retrospect? She'd let those other girls young-love themselves right through their distinct fear of the future—that was her job and nobody else's in the whole damn town. Collar their necks and wrists, leash them, pull the rope tight and wrap it to the headrests. Press her ragged teeth against their musk fur and curse into their bowels. Let them go still as corpses, but then, slowly, Lazarus-like, flesh waking, blood filling lining and lapping, lapping until they're shrieking like enheated beasts, like nothing could punish them more than she could. And then she'd hold them. Against her ribs tight while her spit and wet dried on the backs of their knees. Hold them while they talked on and on about chemistry quizzes or book reports, or "Those aren't wolves, are they?" and she'd reach over the front seat and pop the passenger side door, letting Genghis out into the midst of the fury.

But never again will she be in that Plymouth. From the windowsill today, every day, the eastern prairie is wind-whipped, splattered with rain, the long grass bent and hurting. Those girls would run if they saw her now . . . they *do* see her now. They zoom the asphalt beyond her window. They zoom and zoom, and pretend not to look up at her caged window. They zoom in and out of this sterile room talking about her in third-person. They only touch her because they have to, but they're still scared and that's some sort of a quiet relief . . . isn't it?

She stepped from the truck all business. Genghis struggled over the gearshift, tumbling after. She watched him stretch and yawn, Papa's old green corduroys she wore, the outfit she'd never grow into even though she always pictured she would—wearing that and a bleach-stained, extra-large Polo the old lady got from the thrift store.

There was a wind in Genghis' bowl haircut, and she thought about how it was too late in the year to have such a strong breeze. Could feel it on her unpierced earlobes, and letting it into her lungs she found it still carried a pale scent of thaw rather than that smokiness of impending winter.

Genghis caught it, blinked into the wind. He batted at his mouth with open fingers and weaved away. He halted in front of a boulder, swaying, unzipped his pants. Piss came in sad pulses, dripped down his pant leg. He worked his dick back in and trotted off without zipping up.

Watching him, she felt a migraine cresting. She had terrible headaches in high school, with eye sparks and icy sweats, a hunger eating itself out of her. Her mother blamed her temper, blamed her imagination, saying, "Don't control it, Sweetie, you'll wind up in jail."

"Jail," she'd repeat, not knowing what else to say, as if angst and anger were something abnormal. "Jail, huh?" But now, here with Genghis, she knew what her mother meant: it's all about decoding personal synonyms. It's all about payment.

Genghis stopped, stared at her. He picked at his ear and smiled his uneven smile. Trotted around a bit more making a soft whooping noise. Momentarily she was convinced he was perfectly healthy and shouted, "Hey, what's up? Just had to get away from Mom, get in the mountains, piss on something new? Don't I know, dude!"

He giggled, nodded but didn't look at her. She got so caught in the thought of misdiagnosis that she was just about to load him up and go home, but he spooked a jackrabbit, gave chase. A good go, his big sneakers slapping the ground, but twenty strides in lost his footing, went down windmilling.

Standing gingerly. Grunting. Still smiling through the blood on his lip. He stumbled over and followed her to the truck. She grabbed the gun, walked over to a slab of red rock. Sitting down, there in the wash, she tried to keep her cheek clamped between her teeth while Genghis dropped to his knees, then his side, pressed his broad back against her shins.

Watching his wide, green eyes work back and forth. Watching those thick eyebrows move up and down. Running her fingers across his thighs and side, under his shirt, trying to feel something, anything, but *what*? The muscle was thinning, replacing itself with atrophied tissue, with something more useless but more weighty than mere fat.

Stupid ranchers, it was their fault. Always shooting at Genghis but couldn't get him, shooting at him for chasing livestock. Coming from the city, she got a kick out of watching it. They couldn't hit him. Before he got sick he was faster than he looked, the way he'd lean into it, tongue lolling wolfishly, knuckles to the ground, the physics of his go-speed a near impossibility.

She'd drive them out to find far-flung pastures and she'd keep her eyes sharp for truck dust plumes coming rushing down the county roads. Or until her junior year when Sheriff Nona showed up at school and the man dragged her out of homeroom, said he'd fine her bony ass. "Five hundred bucks." Thumbs in his back pockets, mirrored sunglasses. "You got that kinda money? I know your mama don't. I'll fine you and, if I got to, shoot your retard myself. Ah now, girl, *settle down* now. Unclench those fists. As much as you wanna be, you ain't a boy. Not a chance whippin me. Everybody else may feel sorry for you, may think they know what you went through before you moved to our town, but it's my job to treat you as you are now. Look, it's simple—can't let your freak chase them cattle. Either keep him tied up, clip him, or I'm pullin rank."

So Genghis was way past prime when she let him be neutered. Just couldn't see keeping him tied up or cloistered in their front yard. And she cried, but it was more of a wet rage, eyes knife-flashing, head loud cramped. Then, aftermath—how she's still not certain why she wept over the surgery—not when her parents' divorce never made her. But you've got to understand, she didn't really know the process of it; she was convinced the neutering would turn Genghis female, into something that didn't know the difference between love and sex, hate and selfishness. Turn him into a woman standing in a Nebraska kitchen scratching and blaming without taking any responsibility.

Dr. Denis dished the brutal news not long after. Said the postponement, getting the neutering done that long after his puberty, triggered Genghis' diabetes. Even though he ate less and less each day, and moved less and less, G's last official weigh-in was off the charts. She landed an extra job stocking coke machines, but still they couldn't afford regular insulin.

Genghis knew what had to happen. Turned away, stared straight ahead, but she couldn't get her fingers out of that soft blond hair. For most of their life together, she kept his hair shaggy and, as he aged, his sparse beard natural. He loved the cold, see. When he was just adopted, mewing in the frosty garage, she convinced her mother to let him sleep at the foot of her bed. Wasn't easy, not with her mother certain he'd try to mount her, and "You want a gaggle of retard babies? Want a multiple abortion? You want to pay the rest of your life for a little stupid sympathy? That's the problem with you, just like your goddamn father, all imagination, no *realization*."

Mother going on and on like this until she silenced her with a "So what if he does fuck me, huh? Can't I just blame Papa too?"

Genghis slept at the foot of her bed, but once they moved to the mountains he fell into the habit of waking her at four a.m. to let him out. She would, blasts of brilliant cold smacking her half-naked body so that crawling back in bed felt excruciatingly warm and she slept well knowing that just after dawn, when she'd set off to catch the school bus, calling out his name, Genghis would burst from a snowdrift and escort her all the way to the road.

But Genghis usually only stayed out whole nights when coyotes invaded the yard. Hearing them yapping, he went ballistic. Seeing them out her bedroom window, five or six, and that titan had to get to them like a drowning man. Barking, drooling, bucking a rodeo, she'd release his fleece pajama collar, his great pale head almost white in the moonlight, and he'd lope into the pack, throwing his arms like propellers.

Never worried about him getting injured—Genghis had this thing where within two minutes of a scratch or a bruise he'd forget he even got it. What's hurt if you can't even remember where it came from? Zoom. Zoom. Her mattress smells like warm earth, and, no, see, like the ranchers, the coyotes couldn't do anything to him. Under those big moons, snow bright as day, they'd converge, but Genghis, he'd shake them off like dirt.

When the sun dropped behind the Prongs. When the world began its turn to hard blue. A fingernail moon on the rise in half-glow. She straddled Genghis, her knees in the dirt. He canted his head, grunted. He kissed the thigh of her pants, drooled. She patted the ground, located the cold gun. Nona's .38, and it kicked much harder than she thought it would, but no blood or brain spurted on her cheeks. Only a blue line of smoke exiting the entry wound.

* * *

Is there any waste of time greater than retrospection? Even as you do it the act becomes its own subject. Genghis was so heavy she should have dug the grave, climbed in, called him down, and shot him there. Should have, but didn't. Shot him in the wash below the knoll with a sound like the world breaking. A jerked and sweaty trigger. The lead slug rocketed through his blond fur, shattered the base of his skull, halted the idling traffic of his funny brain.

Or the bullet might have exited his smiling face. This possibility she briefly considered but didn't confirm. Zip—right through his short-term memory and out the fleshy cul-de-sac of his nose . . . maybe? Yes, this sort of thinking is pleasant if kept short, if not investigated, the bullet traveling beyond its original mission and finding another victim, skewering the white belly of an unsuspecting pine squirrel, a little Egyptian-like companion for Genghis' next stop, Mishap Heaven, butter sandwiches and bubble baths.

Then dragging that corpse to the knoll. Easily the most exhausting thing she's ever done—forty-degree slope, twenty feet of talus, wispy dirt, heaving, skinning her knees. Blood thrummed her sinuses. Blood threaded the whites of her eyes. "Come on, Boy," she huffed. "Come on, Buddy."

Gripping those fat, freckled ankles—Jesus, she wouldn't cry, wouldn't. Held her gaze up, chin cocked skyward so she wouldn't accidentally see his face. "Come on, *still a team.*"

Point of death's a vacuum switch—now she knows. Some people claim there's a loss of weight when the soul secedes the flesh, that laboratory hospital beds equipped with scales show six ounces vanishing with a last breath—wrong. She could feel it in her biceps, in the tearing muscles of her narrow, soaking back. Death's a star imploding, a black hole, something physical and inescapable, gathering mass unto itself, wanting more. If not, why's decomposition so goddamn slow?

Halfway up the knoll, Genghis' blond hair and the big lobe of his right ear snagged on a fist of quartz. She tried yanking the caught flesh loose by shaking his legs, getting his head to lull sideways, but his ankles slipped from her damp hands. His feet hit with a clatter of talus.

Maybe pain and violence are the exact opposite of death, some sort of exhaust, just to throw us off?

Taking the moment to catch her breath, straightening up, raising her arms above her head to stretch the shoulders. Adjust her spine. Blink grit from her eyes. *Why would a soul carry weight at death when weight is finally not needed?*

Fewer than ten feet to go, but when she leaned over and again lifted the ankles they were much stiffer, thicker. She had to dig her nails in. Yes, substantially bulkier, to where, surprised, terrified, she almost threw them down. *He's growing—he's still growing?*

No, can't be. Goose bumps sprouting. Fighting them, keeping focus off the reality of the task, turning her mind to the past. Fanatics, scratchy voices in her deep ears, those naysayers Papa loved on Midwestern radio because he refused to buy a TV . . . because it ruined the imagination—

Brothers and Sisters, hear this: Mishaps do not have souls. Mishapping is the ultimate penance, the sin of the father passed on. To accredit a Mishap with even the smallest soul is a gateway ideology to jeremiad platforms, to fundamental miscreantism. Got it? Say with me now, Amen!

Blood rushed to her scalp. Huffing, she jerked the ear free and continued upwards. Her thoughts weren't anger so much as sorrow, just as, even now, strapped face-down—if you can even call it a face—to this mattress, the blood rushing to her scalp isn't what it seems—it's all phantom, as the voice in her head. *And creatures with no souls . . .* but wait, stop, what are you really saying when making such claims, that impulse and spirit have nothing in common?

Five feet to the knoll.

Once on top, she turned Genghis onto his back and dug. When she'd drag him into the grave, he'd be face-up and she'd close her eyes doing it.

* * *

After having spent most of her energy dragging Genghis up to the knoll, and then retrieving the shovel from the truck bed, digging the grave took over an hour. At four feet deep and seven long, she finally pulled him up to it, stood astride the hole, tugged him in.

She didn't know what to do next. Leaned on her shovel like a Zane Grey sketch, watched that same strange breeze whirlpool the hole, twist Genghis' hair. It was dusk, September, her senior year of high school, and caught in that mountainous panorama, caught in night's first cast of hard blue, she could picture Genghis' spirit—something made of light snow—separate from his carcass. Watching it hop easily out of the shallow grave, glance about for direction.

To the east, the valley yawned into sage plains and to the south the great, bare cottonwoods along the Teller River lifted black fingers to the rising moon. But Genghis' soul turned west, trotted off with that big, wide-hip gate, off toward the white teeth of the Prong Peaks, west, a hot run for the tundra and thin, thin air.

This comforted her. They were only kids when her mother moved them to Idaho, and if they'd stayed in Nebraska, in the choked and tangled Lincoln suburbs, in those fenced backyards filled with the skeletons of swing sets and the reek of freshly mowed grass, what motivation for Genghis' spirit then?

She coughed though didn't need to. But maybe it was forcing the cough that finally opened her brain, got her thinking about crying? Thinking that she should cry, you know, that she hadn't since Dr. Denis' diagnosis, and how good it had made her old lady feel seeing her like that. Her mom didn't take her hand off her that whole day, kept feeding her aspirin, the woman's back straight and eyes full of purpose, a purpose like her daughter had finally forgotten Papa.

Problem was she didn't feel like crying.

Standing there over Genghis' grave, she didn't feel much of anything. But something in her said she could really let a storm out if she concentrated. *Maybe go do it for Jenny or Liz or Amber? Or for Mom again? Who'd appreciate it most . . . since I won't?*

And she almost felt guilty about wasting it, but in the end she didn't cry, just got to filling the grave.

"A bone to the dog is not charity."

Jack London said that. She memorized this quote, even considered more than a few times getting it tattooed across her shoulders. Said, "Charity is the bone shared with the dog, when you are just as hungry as the dog."

She wasn't a lesbo. Wasn't a girl. Wasn't a daughter. Wasn't a lover. Wasn't a killer. Was just hungry, always hungrier, but not now—she was filling up, could feel it, and when she had a mound, she patted it proudly with blistered hands.

Next, she gathered large stones, lugged them over, stacked them on the turned earth. Her strength had returned. A refreshing sweat rolled around her eye sockets, down her biceps. Stone after stone, bigger, bigger. She needed a pyramid, a shrine, and the moonlight was good so she just kept stacking—but something happened. Waddling to the grave with a small boulder cradled in the crux of her elbows, with her back straight, her knees bent and butt out, a sudden flurry of thick clouds swept across the sky and cut her light. Then the coyotes wailed. Hundreds of them. And when the uproar hit her ears the boulder rolled out of her arms, thudding and crunching sage, and she pictured them converging, their filthy jaws tearing the skin off in strips, the pop of canines deflating her skull—she started sobbing.

Blindly, torrents, every cell trembling. It wasn't fear, it was . . .

Dragging the shovel, she bolted for the truck only to reach it and realize she didn't have the gun. Nona's .38, not hers to lose. Wiping at her eyes she made out the glint of its hilt, hurried back to swipe it up. The coyotes' wails grew and with them her sobs. Now fishtailing the corners, throwing dust from the front wheels into the cockeyed beams of her truck, head blurred with the clouded windshield, blurred so she couldn't tell the difference between here and there, now and then, before and after. Isn't there hard blue night beyond those headlights? She cocks the hammer. The howls grow louder. Coyotes following, hunting. They have nothing to fear now, but does she still owe the beasts?

She can't take her eyes off the road, can't unlock her left fist from the wheel and the fingers of her right from the revolver. Can't turn her head to see but she knows the passenger seat is completely empty and something, that thing in her, *it* lifts the barrel, wet softness, roof of mouth, metal tapping, rolling, cracking on tooth.

Forest begins two hundred yards upslope from Genghis' knoll, from the grave. The entire setting a species of beautiful that crowds your brain and breeds, eggs in your limbs, in your senses, until you swear it's the only reason your nerve-endings ever existed. Warped junipers dot the hillock, the peach-rock gully, before straightening up and clustering into a black copse of ponderosa and fir, and, beyond them, peeking over their wooded hairline, the magnificent Prongs.

Tonight, after strapping her down to the mattress and folding the wheelchair into the corner, one nurse moves to the window, her fingers on the iron caging, and tries not to weep. She whispers, "Motherfucker, look at all this nothing."

"Come on," the other nurse says, holding open the heavy door, "let's get dolled up, hit the bars, get the boys drooling tonight. I'm hungry."

But the first nurse doesn't move, only shakes her head. She sighs, drops her chin to her chest. She's a lonely woman with a mind that's suddenly too heavy, and right now she's desperately trying to recall the last time she felt loved by someone. Letting her eyes close, she mutters, "This isn't what I signed up for . . ."

"What's that, Sweetie?"

"Keeping dead things alive."

"Yeah," the other says, slipping her big, metal keychain onto her wrist and spinning it like a bracelet, "but it sure beats the alternative."

"What's the alternative?"

"Can't imagine."

The first nurse blinks her eyes open and turns from the window. Rubbing her neck, she frowns at the girl on the mattress. "But what do you think actually happened to this one? Think her father really . . . ?"

"Rumors. Random, corny rumors. Mishaps and retard babies and mothers with guns—people's imaginations. Who knows if her name's even Melinda."

ELLARAINE LOCKIE

Rattle of Recall

The cheatgrass and sage shrouded mound
suggested an ill-kept grave
sized to fit our family of seven
For years my father had refused
to enlighten the dark under it that fed
my fantasies, fat now with funereal drama

It was a white-hot August afternoon
after wheat harvest
when he shed some life on the dead
of the homestead root cellar
My reward for hoeing the walkway weeds

He lifted the wood-weathered door
Laid out flat and worm-holed
like a body awaiting burial
Said he hadn't been down there since I was born
As ten-year entombed air exhaled its cool comfort

He cleared away the spider webs
And with flashlight precision
paved a path past the steep wooden planks
While my budding spider phobia obscured
the reason he held a hoe in his other hand

I stalled on twilight's fringe until farm girl
self-respect urged me over the edge of angst
And I entered the underground pantry
Breathed in the damp and earthy air

Where grandparents banked fall's bounty
from a bygone apple grove and vegetable garden
And where they kept nest eggs cool

beside a wealth of preserved provisions
As well as salads, fresh meats and milk
that stayed chilled until supper

But even before we found the pickle-filled jar
hidden behind an earthenware butter churn
I sensed my grandmother's presence
And her eternal tending of the timbered shelves
that held hundreds of like jars
I traced a finger over the words
chicken-scratched across the yellowed label
1905—*Bread and Butter Pickles*

I felt the calligraphic connection
A fiercely familial cord
As if I belonged to my grandmother
by some umbilical magic that somehow
left my mother barren

So I wasn't afraid when a foreshadow
flickered from the stairwell ledge at eye level
Grandmother confirming contact
I couldn't still the happiness of having her
after sixty years of separation

The mass was too murky to make out in dim light
Way too dwarfed for a grandmother, yet it moved
A companion pet or maybe Grandmother's incarnation
I stepped closer, beckoned by old arms
encircling me, the smell of cinnamon rolls baking
and tales about cottontail rabbits

The envy over my friends with grandmas
elbowed me fearless and forward
But my father flinched at the moving shadow
and like a Great Pyrenees Mountain Dog
defending his flock of sheep

He positioned himself between me and the movement
that was now a nearly immobile coil
A brown and yellow blotched rope
rattling when direct light divulged its identity
before Father beheaded it one-handed with the hoe

The body flipped over and belly-danced its dirge
The arrow-shaped end fell to the dirt floor
The snake's eyes fastened to mine
Held me in their vise
As surely as its jaws had squeezed
the life from many a field mouse

My father's arms enfolded me
with insight and two fitful shakes
Freeing me from the otherworldly trap
And with a look as telling as a grandma's fairy tale
Welcomed me back to the world of fear and phobias
envy and acceptance

He used the hoe to bury the head
A farmer's favor to the vulture
who would have eaten it along with the venom
And he gave the ten hollow grey rattles to me
Reminders of Grandmother's mystical powers
that I preserve in her emptied pickle jar

MICHAEL ENGELHARD

CREATIVE NONFICTION

Blacktop Cuisine

"Dinner is ready, guys." We pull our chairs to the kitchen table as Bart takes a bubbling casserole from the oven. The fragrance of masa, chillies, and cilantro suffuses the room.

"Looks great," I say, forking up my first bite. The meat is a bit stringy, with a gamey tang to it.

"What is it?"

"Bobcat tamales," Bart says. Furry white eyebrows wiggle up his forehead like caterpillars, accentuating the trademark Blankenship smirk.

"Where did you get this, Bart?"

"Oh, outside of Pagosa. At first I thought it was a standard poodle."

"*Hhmmm. . . .* interesting," I say, taking another, more tentative bite. Not what I imagined cat to taste like. And not "like chicken" at all.

My friend and roommate Bart is a latter-day mountain man. He works for Outward Bound and sometimes for an outdoors survival school. With his ex-wife he authored a book about flint knapping and other Stone Age skills. His chert or bottle glass arrowheads are not just functional—they are works of art. He has taught his children to catch trout with bare hands and knows how to weave fishing nets from home-processed yucca fibers. Bart's idea of dressing up for a night on the town is to don his brain-tanned buckskin shirt and pants. I never know what will show up in our freezer from day to day.

Like other aficionados, Bart became a road kill gourmet by default. As the founder of a school for primitive skills, he needed furs, hides, feathers, antlers, and sinew in order to teach tanning, arrow fletching, or tool hafting. Outside of Alaska, highways seemed like the best places to procure these materials. Bart started by calling the Colorado DOT for recent deer kills, and there were usually a few in the Boulder vicinity. Skinning the carcasses, Bart found that much of the meat was still good. A frugal guy who hates waste, he began to take these scraps home. Generally, Bart is not too concerned about ticks, rabies, or Tularemia. He washes his hands and any meat thoroughly and otherwise thinks that a dose of bacteria will keep his immune system strong. When in doubt, he has a surefire way of testing road kill. "I cook a small piece without seasoning and taste it. If it tastes like it was dipped in vinegar then it likely won't make you sick. But my kids won't eat it, and so I leave it."

As a parent of three, with little income, Bart is quick to point out the economic aspect of eating road kill. Since the 1980s, he has supplemented his family's larder with deer, elk, and bobcat. At times, up to a third of the meat consumed by the Blankenships comes from fender benders. At 30–50 pounds of usable meat per deer and a store value of 2–5 dollars per pound, the savings can be substantial. But unlike some of my dirtbag river guide friends, Bart draws the line at dumpster diving, which he considers gross.

A roster of Bart's "trophies" reads like a Who's Who of western wildlife. My friend admits to having boiled and eaten a great horned owl once. "I ran it over and felt I had to do something with it," he says. But generally, he sets aside the "exotics"—coyote, raccoon, fox, opossum, wild hog, otter, badger, and rattlers—to transform them into hatbands, mittens, or arrow quivers.

The legalities, as well as the actual experience, of peeling bunnies off the asphalt can be Byzantine. While Bart dodges traffic to avoid suffering his dinner's fate, he does well to remember federal and state laws. It is illegal, for example, to collect certain animals from the road or elsewhere. Only Native Americans with a religious permit are allowed to possess an eagle feather. The state of Utah issues a permit each time an individual wants to retrieve a killed animal. And whereas motorists in Arizona are entitled to keep meat from a deer they have hit, the same act can land you in prison in Oregon. On long road trips, scrounging can become quite an ordeal. Bart remembers one outing in particular. "We were driving in Kansas and had four raccoons in bags tied to the roof, and they were thawing, and blood was dripping down the windows. We found we weren't allowed to have them in Kansas, even though we picked them up elsewhere. So we ended up beating it back to Colorado where they'd be legal." Another time, Bart's youngest son got carsick and threw up in his seat next to half a fox his dad was transporting. On the bright side, the mess got them out of a citation for speeding.

Even at his home, the Law keeps an eye on Bart's preparations. He recalls the time a concerned neighbor alerted the authorities. "The EPA came and asked where our toxic chemicals were for tanning the hides. When we showed them the buckets of brains, they said we might want to keep a lid on to keep out the flies. The Department of Wildlife came while we were using a ceiling fan to dry some furs, but they left with a brochure of our primitive skills school. The fire department came when we smoked hides but went away when they saw the smoke coming out of our wood stove and going straight into a deer hide. The City of Boulder came and left, and so did the police."

While Bart may strike some people as eccentric or a throwback to fur rendezvous times, more and more Americans are discovering the potential of road kill. Taxidermists fix flattened pelts for natural history museum exhibits. A gallery owner in South Dakota plucks porcupine quills to fashion into jewelry. A New Mexico sculptress and tattoo artist assembles bones into motorcycles or "Gnarleys." An Arizona state biologist prepares skulls and other skeletal parts to be used as educational kits in schools. Frozen corpses serve him as models for scientific illustrations; fresher meat ends up on the barbecue grill or feeding his boas and pythons.

Despite their entertainment value and utility, creative uses of road kill can hardly disguise the social and ecological costs incurred daily on U.S. highways. Aside from abetting habitat fragmentation, pollution, or noise, roads take a more direct and bloody toll on biodiversity. Vehicles kill hundreds of millions of animals every year. Snakes and amphibians—including many endangered species—take the brunt of this assault. Not even our National Parks are safe. On Yellowstone's roads alone, 1,559 large mammals died between 1989 and 2003. To wit, the boundary between victims and perpetrators becomes blurred. Two hundred people died last year in about 250,000 collisions with animals. The average repair of an automobile damaged by deer (or more specifically, by reckless driving) runs around two thousand dollars.

Perhaps, like our fellow creatures, we humans are not hardwired for life in the fast lane. Neither, some critics insist, were we meant to eat carrion.

Simply the thought of consuming possum paella or rattlesnake ragout will induce dry heaves in most people. Yet the widespread prejudice against scavenging only masks humble origins. It is a credo, a pretense akin to the convert's denial of obsolete pagan practices. The vile reality may be hard to stomach: Gleaning is in our genes. It helped us become who we are.

The concept of Man the Hunter (and by extension Woman the Gatherer) is not entirely the product of gender biases ruling science or politics. It also appears as a case of myth-making by a species in search of dignity, a species still largely intent on seeing itself as the apex of—if not separated from—the animal kingdom. *Nature* is red in tooth and claw; *we* are sticklers for table manners, devotees of fancy cooking. Truth be told, rather than wielding spears and skewering African mammoths, *Homo sapiens* began its career as a beggar in Nature's soup kitchen. Opportunists to the bone, our hominid ancestors on the savanna stuffed their faces with leftovers wrangled from lion or leopard kills, in competition with hyenas, jackals, and vultures. In an eat-or-be-eaten world, bone picking proved to be more efficient than gathering (especially when protein yield is compared), yet less risky than hunting—an optimal foraging strategy. In this scenario, the invention of stone tools literally gave us an edge over other scavengers by facilitating dismemberment, as well as marrow and brain extraction. (Which can be tough with fingernails and underdeveloped dentition.) Speech and cooperation followed suit, in turn giving birth to more complex behaviors like big game hunting and presidential campaigning.

Supposedly, anthropology can even shed light on the rank reputation of blacktop cuisine. Evolutionary psychologists speculate that our revulsion at eating dead and rotten things (as opposed to just rotten things, like Limburger cheese) developed as an adaptive trait. This sort of "intuitive microbiology" helped early *Homo* to avoid lethal cases of food poisoning. Physical anthropologists, on the other hand, like to point out that even under an equatorial sun, it can take up to 48 hours until flesh begins to putrefy. Furthermore, carcasses produced by "natural" death are likely to be free of dangerous parasites because most such deaths result from malnutrition rather than from disease. Good news for the harvesters of ditches and interstates, I guess.

In my home state, Alaska, the road kill menu is less varied than Bart's backyard fare. As if to compensate, everything is super-sized here, including the servings. (An adult 1,100-pound moose normally yields about 700 pounds of meat, meat that is much leaner and more nutritious than beef.) Trains and vehicles annihilate about 820 moose per annum, carnage only surpassed in Sweden, where motorists cull moose populations by 4,000–6,000 animals each year. About 120 Alaskan moose annually fall prey to the Alaska Railroad's yellow-and-blue engines. With a sense of humor honed at 50 degrees below zero, residents of this state call the train between Fairbanks and Anchorage "the Moose Butcher." When northern lights play above snowdrifts, animals follow the plowed tracks as substitutes for easy trails. Allegedly, bull moose even take on locomotives—as they would rack-sporting competitors—during the fall rut. Heavy snowfalls and overcrowding can drive moose into urban areas, leading to an increase in fatalities. Occasionally, the quick hand of technology also cuts short the lives of black bears, Dall's sheep, and mountain goats. Sixteen-hour nights and icy roads result in tons of high-quality food-stuff: prime cuts, tender loin, spare ribs, and minced meat. And at subarctic temperatures, this bonanza does not spoil easily.

Alaska's urban and semi-urban centers have therefore implemented pro-grams to retrieve and distribute road kill to the needy. In Anchorage, Fair-banks, the Matanuska-Susitna Valley, and on the Kenai Peninsula, hundreds of charities and individuals benefit from low visibility, speeding, drunk driv-ing, and poor road conditions. Nearly all road kill moose in the state goes to nonprofit organizations, many of which are churches. Beneficiaries must respond within thirty minutes to a coordinator's call to salvage the meat. If they fail to do so, the follower-up on a list will be given a chance. Alaska Fish and Game biologists or hunters affiliated with the nonprofits often are called upon to shoot wildlife injured in accidents.

Eileen Brooks is the road kill coordinator for the Anchorage region and Mat-Su Borough of south-central Alaska. Colleagues refer to her as the "Queen of the Gut Pile." But according to Eileen, the Blankenship diet helps alleviate hardship in a place where the cost of living is high. "A lot of people can't af-ford to buy steaks or even hamburger," she says. And while many Alaskans enjoy the fruits of subsistence hunting and fishing, that venue is barred to the urban poor. In Eileen's area alone, one hundred nonprofits are signed up for road kill in a typical winter, and some community churches receive an average of ten moose a year.

A major tenet of sustainable living admonishes us not just to recycle but also to curb wastefulness in the first place. Unfortunately, a society obsessed with driving is unlikely to ever fully embrace measures that reduce wildlife mortality on its roads. Speed limits, better signage, fencing, or animal crosswalks all could prevent unnecessary deaths. Tight budgets and narrow minds, however, ensure that ecological attrition will continue. Short of all-out solutions, we can at least honor the casualties with a token gesture. Sharing the mangled flesh in a form of unholy communion, we acknowledge their sacrifice. So, let us show some respect. Let us neaten our highways a bit. Let us break the mold of culinary routine. To connoisseurs sick of French, Thai, or Mexican, Bart recommends the chef's special: grille gopher in crankcase oil with a side of creamed coyote—guaranteed to tickle the palate while sparing the wallet. (Do yourselves a favor, though, and skip the muskrat mush.)

Bon appétit!

C. R. RESETARITS

Ocotillo

Desert meadow
ballerinas
in fifth position

moon caught
monsoon released
full corps staging

sway, turn
pricked pirouette
flame blooms tipping

fingers in this
land of odd quivers
and skyward arms.

Or ancient occupants
of open, stony
of desert slopes.

Bajada
ocotillo
are firebirds, are

lunar troops
arms raised
to heaven

are archers,
flame fingered
earth arcing

are weird warriors,
curious creatures stirred
by summer's sky-slit rains.

LANCE NIZAMI

Ludlow, California

"EATS" declares the rooftop sign, in letters pink, sun-bleached from red

Each letter's shape is lined by thin gray broken neon tubing
Those tubes remain unlit and gray, their glamourous glare burned out
    long years ago
Now, tourists turn off-highways just to see what dead words look like

Death is fast, decay is slow—here, in dry clear semi-desert air

Once, the human life seemed permanent
It came from wetter lands, and back to wetter lands it went, retired
It left behind some signs that life had thrived here once-upon-a-time:

"EATS" declares the rooftop sign, in letters pink, sun-bleached from red.

WENDY VIDELOCK

Where the Squirrel Lay Dead,

a riot of crows
breaking bread.

AMY BRUNVAND

ESSAY

Green Jell-O for the *Genius Loci* or How to Save the Earth with Poetry

Can poetry save the Earth?[1] Frankly I think it's a splendid idea.[2] Lately I've spent quite a lot of time out in the streets trying to save the Earth,[3] and it's clear to me that there has been a communications breakdown. The potential for catastrophic environmental crisis is making our present situation increasingly dicey, yet it often seems like the wrong people are trying to address the problems in various unhelpful ways. Citizen concerns go unheard by corporate-sponsored elected officials who seem to be either actually baffled or deliberately obtuse about scientific data.[4] Some people like Sverker Sörlin[5] believe the key to crossing this communication barrier lies with the humanities because, as he wrote in the scholarly journal *BioScience*, "We cannot dream of sustainability unless we start to pay more attention to the human agents of the planetary pressure that environmental experts are masters at measuring but that they seem unable to prevent."[6] The founders of a new Australian journal called *Environmental Humanities* call for putting this human focus to practical use: "The environmental humanities is necessarily, therefore, an effort to inhabit a difficult space of simultaneous critique

---

1 Felstiner, John. *Can poetry save the earth?: A field guide to nature poems.* Yale University Press, 2009.
2 Brunvand, Amy. "More Poets, Fewer Lawyers." Canyon Country Zephyr August 3, 2014. HTTP://WWW.CANYONCOUNTRYZEPHYR.COM/2014/08/03/MORE-POETS-FEWER-LAWYERS-POEMS-BY-AMY-BRUNVARD/
3 I'm the woman in orange pants waving a banner on the Salt Lake City federal courthouse steps in the documentary *Wrenched (2014).*
4 Particularly regarding things like global climate change that they don't want to understand.
5 Apparently everyone in Sweden has names like that.
6 Sörlin, Sverker. "Environmental Humanities: Why Should Biologists Interested in the Environment Take the Humanities Seriously?" *BioScience* 62.9 (2012): 788–89.

and action."[7] Sounds good to me. The world needs saving. Poetry to the rescue!

But, how poetic does this Earth-saving poetry actually need to be? After all, one of the truly great Earth-saving poems is The Lorax.[8] Likewise Publishers Weekly derided the poems of Edward Abbey as "cornball," "overwritten," "doggerel-like," and "Victorian in sentiment," and said that they "may interest Abbey's fans, but not poetry readers."[9] Touché. But clearly we have a problem, here. In order for poetry to save the Earth, someone besides poetry readers has to read it.

One possible solution lies in "relocalization" which is one of the central tenets of the sustainability movement and which you can think of as a kind of survivalist movement for people who are not actually crazy.[10] People are attracted to reading about familiar places, and they might like place-based poems. I live in Utah, ergo I should begin my search for poetry to save the Earth by constructing a poetic ecology to save Utah. In any case, love of place is a convincing argument in favor of conservation, and Utah exerts a distinctly odd pull on the human spirit. One theory has it that susceptible souls are sucked toward a gravitational anomaly located directly under the Mormon temple;[11] another theory holds that ancient rock art carved on sandstone walls in remote desert canyons opens a portal to an alternate reality.[12] In any case, people who try to move to Utah from elsewhere often run screaming as if chased by a furious genius loci,[13] and Utah natives who try to leave snap back into place entirely against their will as if attached by a giant bungee cord.

On the map, Utah is not a conceptually complicated place. Lyons & Williams have the essential geographical outline.[14] All Utah is divided into three

---

7 Rose, Deborah Bird, et al. "Thinking through the Environment, Unsettling the Humanities." *Environmental Humanities*. 1 (2012): 1–5.

8 Seuss, Dr. *The Lorax*. New York: Random House, 1971.

9 "Earth Apples = (Pommes Des Terre) The Poetry of Edward Abbey." *Publishers Weekly* 241, no. 30 (July 25, 1994): 44.

10 e.g. Quilley, Stephen. "Transition Skills," in *Handbook of Sustainability Literacy*. Arran Stibbe, ed. UIT Cambridge Ltd., 2009.

11 The temple is situated at the mathematical origin of a massive Cartesian grid that overlays the entire state.

12 See various issues of "Proceedings of the Utah Rock Art Research Association," UTAHROCKART. ORG.

13 Much like the one that chased Napoleon out of Russia in *War and Peace*.

14 Lyon, Thomas, and Terry Tempest Williams, eds. *Great & Peculiar Beauty: A Utah Reader*. Layton, UT: Gibbs Smith, 1995.

parts: the "Great Basin" which includes Great Salt Lake, the West Desert and the Greatest Snow on Earth®; The Colorado Plateau home to Utah's iconic red-rock desert; and the Uinta Mountains where you may find conventional picture-postcard lakes, forests and wildlife.[15] Two largish rivers—the Green and the Colorado—run through the landscape like the two essential kinds of chili, and their confluence lies at the mystic Heart of Redrock[16] in the center of Canyonlands National Park. The geological substrate is generally exposed everywhere, but here and there rocks are overlain by a veneer of biological and/or human activity. Most of Utah's human population lives in a sprawling urban area along the Wasatch Front between two mountain ranges that trap urban pollution in a cold-sink known (not at all fondly) as "The Inversion"[17] which renders breathing toxic for weeks at a time. The rest of the state is largely small-town, rural or completely unpopulated since more than half of the land is managed by various federal government agencies.[18] The state capitol, Salt Lake City, is also the world headquarters of the Church of Jesus Christ of Latter Day Saints (a.k.a. Mormons), and Utah's population may be conveniently divided into "Us" (Mormons) and "Them" (everyone else). Utah legislators[19] are heard in the marble halls of the capitol building addressing each other as "brother" and "sister" to affirm their affiliation with "Us." As for minorities, Polynesians, successfully recruited by "The Church," typically affiliate with "Us"; Hispanics and Native Americans (Ute, Paiute, Goshute, Shoshone and Diné) tend to affiliate with "Them."

So that's the basic outline. The next problem is to find poetry to match the scenery;[20] then it's a simple matter of pinning the poems on a map. So let's start with what is probably the best-known poetry contest in Utah—the annual Jell-O Haiku Contest that has been sponsored by the Salt Lake Tribune newspaper since 2007. Jell-O was named the official state snack by the Utah

---

15 Though due to a tectonic glitch the Uintas trend perpendicular to continental drift.
16 Not to be confused with the *Heart of Darkness*.
17 Similarly, citizens of Denver have anthropomorphized their pollution layer as "The Brown Cloud."
18 A situation that drives libertarians, sagebrush rebels, and other worshipers of private property literally insane.
19 Mormon Republicans, for the most part.
20 To paraphrase Wallace Stegner.

Legislature in 2001,[21] "whereas Utah has been the number one per capita consumer of Jell-O brand gelatin for many years."[22] During the 2002 Olympics a green Jell-O pin (with many variations) was the hot souvenir item, and political cartoonist Pat Bagley contributed a glow-in-the-dark radioactive green Jell-O pin to the mix in order to protest various ill-advised nuclear waste storage schemes proposed for Utah's West Desert. In 2006 when my ex-husband Brian was running as the sacrificial Democratic candidate for U.S. Congress he wore Bagley's nuclear Jell-O pin on his lapel[23] to remind people that the sitting congressman Rob Bishop (R-UT-1) was a former lobbyist for the Envirocare nuclear waste disposal facility in the West Desert and that he (Bishop) had just voted in favor of resuming nuclear testing at the Nevada Nuclear Test Site.[24] In order to reinforce public awareness of this transgression, Brian and I spent quite a lot of other people's money to televise a political ad that featured a mushroom cloud followed by an image of ourselves holding our exceptionally cute, blonde baby.[25] Well, as I said, Brian failed to win so he donated his remaining campaign funds to Peter Corroon[26] who was running for mayor of Salt Lake County and, due to the sudden implosion of his opponent's campaign,[27] found himself unexpectedly the front-runner. In his subsequent two terms as Salt Lake County Mayor, Corroon not only vastly improved bicycle infrastructure in the County but had a generally stellar environmental record in other respects as well. What's more, not long after all this took place Congressman Bishop did the one and only visionary thing he has ever done[28] by establishing a Cedar Mountains Wilderness Area in order to block transportation routes to the aforemen-

---

21 S.R. 5 (2001) "Resolution Urging Jell-O Recognition."

22 Particularly the lime-green variety mixed with shreds of carrot, though this is merely common knowledge not encoded in law.

23 Next to a tiny American flag, of course.

24 Despite the fact that fallout from such tests is hazardous to human health and due to prevailing winds tends to fall largely on people in Utah. Hence the term "downwinders" to refer to those affected.

25 A sly nod to the infamous "Daisy" ad aired by LBJ during the 1964 U.S. presidential election.

26 A first cousin of former Vermont governor Dr. Howard Dean, famous for the "Dean Scream" that may or may not have undermined his presidential candidacy.

27 Ethical concerns emerged after County Mayor Nancy Workman hired her own daughter as a "ghost employee" paid with public funds.

28 At least as far as I can remember.

tioned proposed nuclear waste dump in Skull Valley.[29] So by squinting just a bit it seems possible to believe that that Jell-O haiku may indeed have played a significant role in Utah's environmental public dialog, even if it was in a six-degrees-of-Kevin-Bacon kind of way.[30]

Radioactive Jell-O, by the way, is a good example of "Mondo Utah" which is the name filmmaker Trent Harris gave to the genius loci of Utah.[31] Mondo Utah exists as a kind of ecotone between the spiritually sublime and inexcusably ridiculous and often manifests on an unexpectedly grand scale. In 2013 Mondo Utah was chosen as the theme of an exhibit at the Utah Museum of Contemporary Art, and the show's curator, out-of-state transplant Aaron Moulton,[32] called Utah "the most spiritual place I've ever been to in my life."[33] Indeed, the mythologies of Mormonism are a prime example of Mondo Utah.[34] Other examples include the discovery of cold fusion by University of Utah chemists, the Mark Hoffman "white salamander" forgeries and bombings, and the salvation of the 2002 Winter Olympics by the weirdly robotic polygamist-descendant and future GOP presidential candidate Mitt Romney. Robert Smithson's artwork Spiral Jetty is both an example of and an artistic response to Mondo Utah. However, Mondo Utah is not all fun and games. It also has a propensity toward flamboyant boondoggles and environmentally catastrophic scams like the government subsidized uranium mining frenzy of the 1950s, the Glen Canyon Dam, the MX Missile, the Central Utah Water Project, and the Tar Sands Triangle[35] which is currently threatening to disappear the entire state in a vast dusty pit.

But back to poetry. Ever since 1935 the Utah State Poetry Society has been publishing a decennial collection called Utah Sings.[36] Back in the '30s Utah's

---

29 This was not actually Bishop's own idea. James V. Hansen who held the seat prior to Bishop had a far more devious mind, and he was the one who thought it up. But let's give credit where credit is due. Bishop is the one who actually passed the legislation.

30 "Six degrees of Kevin Bacon" is a game in which players try to link any Hollywood actor living or dead to Kevin Bacon. The film Footloose (1984) starring Kevin Bacon was filmed in Lehi, Utah.

31 Harris, Trent. Mondo Utah. Salt Lake City, UT: Dream Garden Press, 1996.

32 Who lasted a little over a year in Utah before he ran screaming.

33 Means, Sean P. "Preview: An 'Anti-Biennial' Takes over UMOCA." Salt Lake Tribune (5/6/2013).

34 See Plan 10 From Outer Space (1997).

35 A distant cousin of the better-known Bermuda Triangle.

36 Utah State Poetry Society. Utah Sings. Utah State Poetry Society, 1935–. Vol. Published every 10 years starting with v.1, 1935.

population was not much above 500,000 souls, and the official State Road Commission map warned travelers to "Carry Water" on the road to Hanksville lest they die of thirst stranded out in the desert.[37] Sentimental capital "N" Nature poetry was in style, and the poems in Utah Sings are about what you'd expect: World War I veteran Andrew M. Anderson ("Night on Timpanogos") finds himself atop a peak in the Wasatch range writing "Here in ultimate peace, and supreme beauty— / I feel so close to God"; Jessie Miller Robinson ("Great Salt Lake") calls a migratory bird habitat of critical global importance, "Sterile, passionless, bitter"; William F. Hansen ("Fading Day (Indian Songs)") pictures the native people, "Skulking, submitting, dying / Soon away, away, goodbye."[38] Once in a while a ray of hope for ecological awareness shines through: Harrison R. Merril ("Jest Sage-Brush") openly confesses, "I love sage-brush! / And all the valleys love it, / Because, like foil around our precious heirlooms, / It preserves for them—and us— / The very fragrance of life's high romance." Nowadays, of course, the Sagebrush Sea is one of the most endangered ecosystems in North America[39] and Utah Governor Gary Herbert is actively trying to devise ways to undermine the Endangered Species Act in order to prevent sage grouse from being listed.[40] Perhaps Herbert could be swayed toward a more pro-sagebrush attitude by reading Mr. Merril's heartfelt poem.

Clearly one problem with such antique poetry is that it was written before the consciousness-raising environmental movement of the 1970s which brought out a new activist streak in many poets. For instance, in America's bicentennial year some overtly activist poems about Utah by David Milton appeared in the scientific journal Environment.[41] The poetry is, how shall we say, pretty bad. For instance, in "Magna" Milton imagines his own body as the Kennecott copper smelter, "A dark phallus stands against the sunset / Spewing its sperm of death." Astonishingly, the Communications Director at Kennecott took the time to write a rebuttal which was published in the

37 Utah State Road Commission. Road Map of Utah. 1947.
38 Even though, judging by his biography, Mr. Hansen actually kind of liked his Ute neighbors.
39 Davies, Kirk W., et al. "Saving the Sagebrush Sea: An Ecosystem Conservation Plan for Big Sagebrush Plant Communities." Biological Conservation 144.11 (2011): 2573–84.
40 O'Donoghue, Amy Joi. "Gov. Gary Herbert: Threat of sage grouse endangered species listing is real, could cost Utah billions." Deseret News, 2/18/2014.
41 Milton, David. "Regarding Creation." Environment 18.4 (1976): 19–20.

Letters to the Editor column declaring that the smelter " . . . is not, I repeat not responsible for the pollution in Salt Lake City" and calling a comment attached to the poem "Irresponsible journalism" and "counterproductive to providing clean air."[42] So whatever you think of his poetic talent, as far as getting a reaction from actual industrial polluters, Mr. Milton has set a high bar for ecopoets everywhere.

But still, considering the many environmental threats to Utah's well-being, there seems to be less Utah ecopoetry lying around than you'd expect. Even though a number of literary Journals are published in Utah,[43] many of them don't seem to have any particular regional focus. The new journal Saltfront refers to the Dark Mountain Project[44] and has an Environmental Humanities mission[45] but they've only published two issues to date. Weber, which has a deeper backfile, looks promising—it has "Contemporary West" right there in the subtitle—but seems a bit thin as far as poetic critique and action. Kimra Perkins[46] mentions some specific features in Arches National Park, and likewise Nancy Takacs[47] imagines hiking to fancifully-named places listed in a guidebook,[48] but they don't stray far from the usual tourist routes. David Lee's,[49] "Nocturne Chinle Strata" (2007) is oddly noncommittal. The Chinle formation contains radioactive petrified wood that lured money-hungry prospectors funded by government subsidies to spider web Utah's wilderness with dirt tracks all leading straight to the Chinle formation and their own radon-gas-poisoned demise; Georgia O'Keefe painted, the Chinle formation, for heaven's sake! But all Lee comes up with is: "Pangea splits

---

42 "Letters." *Environment* 18.8: 44.

43 The ones I know about are listed here in reverse alphabetical order with the acronym of any affiliated institution of higher education: *Western Humanities Review* (U of U), *Weber: The Contemporary West* (WSU), *Touchstones* (UVU), *Sugar House Review, Saltfront, Quarterly West* (U of U), *Petroglyph* (USU, RIP), *Isotope* (USU, RIP), *Irreantum: a Review of Mormon Literature and Film, Enormous Rooms* (U of U), *Ellipsis* (Westminster).

44 HTTP://DARK-MOUNTAIN.NET/.

45 "*Saltfront* is an arts and literary journal for a radically new type of ecological storytelling. We are searching for the newest and most vibrant eco-lyrical expressions, new ways to tell stories of what it means to be human amidst the monumental ecological transformations taking place on this planet." Saltfront.org.

46 *A Desert Guide*, 1986.

47 *Domes and Pinnacles*, 1999.

48 Pretty obviously Allen, Steve. *Canyoneering the San Rafael Swell*. Salt Lake City, UT: University of Utah Press, 1992.

49 About whom more later.

into continents / which float, collide, grind, erupt." Oh, here we go! Claudia Putnam's[50] poem "Global Warming Scenarios: Rocky Mountain Region" (2007) takes environmental issues head-on with an elegy for the extinction of snow, aspen, pikas, glaciers, and trout, and it's poetry in action too: Western Resource Advocates reprinted her poem on their blog Sept 20, 2012.[51] True, Putnam used to work for WRA, but still it is encouraging that someone hoped the poem might exert an influence on public dialog.

Let's see what our Utah poet Laureates have to say. There have been four of them since Utah started its Poet Laureate program in 1997: David Lee (1997),[52] Kenneth W. Brewer (2003), Katherine Coles (2006), and Lance Larsen (2012).[53] Oh, look here! After Lee[54] retired from his faculty position at Southern Utah University he published a collection called So Quietly the Earth[55] dedicated to Ken [Seldom Seen][56] and Jane Sleight; the librarian who catalogued it, classified it as "Human Ecology—Poetry." And here it is! Exactly the kind of poem I'm looking for! "Paragonah Canyon—Autumn," rage, rage against the senseless environmental destruction of the Utah landscape! "Alas. Poor Utah. / Weep for Utah. / So far from Heaven. / So terribly close to California." You go, Mr. Lee.

So it's not quite as simple as I hoped, this business of saving the Earth with poetry. It's easy enough to find Nature poetry gushing with love for the landscapes and people of Utah, and this is essential of course because, "In the end we will conserve only what we love," [57] but however much critique they offer, Nature poems strike me as lacking in action. Somebody needs to rile up those poets and encourage them to vent a bit,[58] but it seems to me that an even bigger obstacle to poetry saving the Earth is that ecopoetry is just too

---

50 Though she's actually from Colorado, not Utah.
51 Putnam, Claudia. "Global Warming Scenarios: Rocky Mountain Region." *Western Views: Words from Western Resource Advocates* 2012/9/20. [Blog post].
52 Best known for rustic pig-oriented humor.
53 Whose latest poetry collection is actually titled *Genius Loci*, University of Tampa Press, 2013.
54 Remember him?
55 Lee, David. *So Quietly the Earth*. Port Townsend, WA: Copper Canyon Press, 2004.
56 Stiles, Jim. "Ken Slight." *Canyon Country Zephyr*. Aug/Sept (1999). Web.
57 Attributed to a speech by Baba Dioum of Senegal at the Tenth General Assembly of IUCN, New Delhi, India, 24 November–1 December 1969, but it's kind of hard to verify since volume I of Proceedings (addresses and speeches) was never published.
58 Maybe the folks at *Saltfront* are doing that.

darned hard to find tucked away in low Google-ranked websites, academic literary journals and various unreviewed small-press books that don't look like they've been checked out of the library for years. Poetry needs to jump out more, swell up in unexpected places, strike people with a new way of looking at things. I suppose a knowledgeable scholar could pull together a wonderful Mondo Utah poetic anthology of environmental rage and action[59] but somebody[60] would need to read through a heck of a lot of poetry in order to find the really great nuclear Jell-O poems, phallic smokestack poems, tragic-pika-extinction poems, angry-at-the-clueless-rural-idiots poems, downwinder poems, and all that other blessed poetic unrest and rage. And then who would read it besides the usual suspects? I'm afraid that by the time Environmental-Humanities Man arrives it will be too late. If this strategy is going to work we need a poetic action of immediate witness, thrusting poetry right into the middle of the conversational spotlight where it can roll up its sleeves and get to work. I have to say, the dour-faced Utah Governor Gary Herbert has always struck me as someone who could use a little more poetry in his life. I think I'll start by sending him that sage-brush poem from the 1930s and then take it from there.

---

59 Something like, Delanty, Greg, ed. *So Little Time: Works and Images for a World in Climate Crisis*. Brattleboro, VT: Green Writers Press, 2014.
60 Maybe me, but I expect it would be have to be somebody with fancier literary credentials.

MICHAEL LUIS DAURO

I slug whiskey spirits . . .

I slug whiskey spirits & marvel the wrinkled minutes of the blue devil crickets. All the livelong night a commingling of commiserations, they & me & the dune owl's croon. I blow a rum tongue ditty from the lip of an empty bottle. I feel right foul. I smell like shit. Bewildered & witching for calamity, aurora. & ain't an owl a Sunday ruin jarred & feathered. Or a moon-eyed lantern runed & clever—taloned, tender. & if this here owl be holy in her loneliness, why do I suffer the cellar door hounds? They call it wasteland. Yet rife life is found even in this here grief-shot desert: the dew upon the cattle skulls, midnights marbled by the snail's silvered journey, armadillos roly-polyed by a bobcat, the chubby jade of an ancient aloe & the cure-alls housed inside. There ain't a woman alive who ain't carrying a desert in her, who ain't been made to feel she's got to keep it tucked away like a badland or whoresome wilderness. & this owl perched upon the saguaro's nettled shoulder ain't an omen, but a sister.

MARLENE OLIN

CREATIVE NONFICTION

Laughter Yoga

Seven hundred bucks for an airplane ticket. Seven days scratched out on the calendar. Rock climbing. Mountain biking. Hiking. I was vacationing with a doppelganger, a *me* nobody knew.

"We raise goats," said RayAnn. "We practice yoga. It'll be the best week ever. Promise."

Years ago, in another life, I met RayAnn at college. English majors, we smoked pot and wrote poetry in smoke-filled rooms. We painted our lips white and our eyes coal black. We were the epitome of cool.

Then life happened. After graduation I moved back home to Miami. Instead of becoming a writer, I married my high school sweetheart and became a stay-at-home mom. I spent the next twenty years cooking, cleaning, changing diapers, waiting for repairmen, helping with homework, wiping noses, carpooling, waiting for more repairmen, driving to the orthodontist, teaching my kids how to drive. My life had become a *Good Housekeeping* cliché.

"Come visit the Tetons!" said RayAnn. "Fresh air. Lots of exercise. You'll get rebooted. You'll start writing again."

While I boomeranged back to my hometown, RayAnn had lived like a nomad. She moved from city to city, teaching mostly at community colleges, managing to get two novels published. She lived the life we had always talked about. One romantic liaison after another. Free and uncommitted. And her stories always ended on a high note as well. Against overwhelming odds, her heroines found happiness. During the six-hour plane ride, I read nonstop.

Sitting on a Dream: Mavis is paralyzed in a car accident. Thanks to the intervention and very hands-on caring of a small-town doctor, she regains the use of her arms and legs. The climax of the book takes place on their honeymoon. Cannons fire and fireworks burst. The book sold twenty thousand copies online alone.

Hotel Hospice: Lorelei has terminal ovarian cancer. Lincoln, her only child, is fifteen years old and has an IQ of one fifty. A promising violinist, he steals manhole covers in his spare time. He's the kind of kid who's either going to end up playing Carnegie Hall or trolling the streets. Then grandpa comes to town. Lorelei's father abandoned her, beat her mother, and stole all their money. But life's all about the second chances. And grandpa has talents no one—NOT EVEN HE!!!—suspects.

"We'll be landing in a few minutes," says the pilot. "It's usually a bumpy ride around now." I shove the two paperbacks into my purse and brace myself. Below me snow-covered peaks puncture the stratosphere. I suck in air to make the plane lighter and lift myself in the seat.

It's a small airport. Lilliputian small. I get off the plane and walk down a flight of stairs to the tarmac. The sky's blindingly blue and cloudless. We're ringed by the Tetons. They're so huge they're one dimensional. For a moment I feel like an actor in a play, the mountains a stage prop, the moon a Cheshire grin.

The people seem unreal, too. Everyone looks the same. Blue-eyed and sun-bleached hair. Tanned and toned. As soon as I find my way to the luggage area, I crane my neck for RayAnn. I figure she'll recognize me first. I'm just an older, weathered version of the college coed I used to be. Brown frizzy hair. Splotchy skin. I might as well be wearing a sign. *Jewish Housewife from Miami.*

"There you are," she says. No, her Facebook page wasn't photoshopped. RayAnn still looks around twenty. Yes, she competed in an Ironman last year. Yes, she really does raise goats.

"It's for weed control," she tells me. "They love thistle. So instead of using weed-killer, we bring my goats to people's yards. They eat the bad stuff and leave the good behind."

We bump along a dirt road and stop in front of a log cabin. It truly is a log cabin. Like on the pancake syrup bottle. Somewhere I hear a rooster crow. The air smells like Christmas. My skin starts to itch.

"We use the old outhouse as a root cellar," says RayAnn. "We've got indoor plumbing, the Internet, the whole shebang."

The walls are covered with New-Agey art. A hand with an eye. A web of yarn with feathers. Though her conversation is peppered with words like *spirit* and *feelings*, there are no periods or pauses, no intake of air. Sentences spill like an avalanche. *We get up at five don't forget there's coffee. We feed the livestock grab some gloves at the door. We do our chores before sunrise don't you love to watch the sun rise isn't the sunrise awesome?*

And she talks as if she has an invisible companion or partner, only no one else is there. No photographs on the fireplace mantel. No his and hers towels. I'm used to tripping over my kids' sneakers and finding Rob's underwear on the floor. There's not a lick of dust in the house.

"We keep our jackets in the closet and our shoes by the door," says RayAnn. When I drop my purse on the couch, she picks it up. "Clutter in the house makes for clutter in the soul."

She's become the nature Nazi. The Fuhrer in the dell. She opens the door to the fridge.

"Help yourself," says RayAnn. It looks like a bank vault and takes up half her kitchen. "We just eat local. Local fruit. Local veggies." When she opens the door to the freezer, I could swear I see a hoof. "We've gotten friendly with a few hunters. They stock us in venison for the year."

I still suffer PTSD from *Bambi*. The forest fire. The mother dying. Who could forget? The sandwich I ate on the plane flips.

She directs me to one of the two bedrooms. It's Martha Stewart pretty. A bed with a blocky quilt. A bathroom with a claw tub and billowing curtains. "This is wonderful," I tell her. It must be fifty degrees in the cabin, and as the sun sets, the temperature's dropping. In Miami, it's sweater weather. In Wyoming, it's a typical summer. My teeth chatter. I crave my flannel night-gown—the one I left home in a drawer.

RayAnn counts down on her fingers. "Monday's hiking, Tuesday's biking, Wednesday's yoga. Once our bodies embrace positive energy, our minds will relax."

She disappears into the kitchen and I hear cabinet doors opening and closing. Meanwhile I unpack and take a closer look at the house. There's not a TV in sight. Her bookshelves are lined with *Sitting on a Dream* and *Hotel Hospice*. A few Tony Hillermans and Louis L'Amours. What ever happened to Kerouac and Corso? The RayAnn I used to know has become a stranger and this stranger is getting stranger by the minute. We are stranded in a wooden shed in the middle of nowhere. We are starting to panic.

Days pass. The two of us develop a routine. Like a shark, RayAnn needs to get moving. My job is to stay out of her way. When she's not tending to her goats, RayAnn's running up mountains, paddling a kayak through the rapids, riding her bike over moguls of Queen Anne's lace. Most of the time I stay home swinging in her hammock, listening to the ripple of her creek. I read. I write. Even so RayAnn is grateful for the company. I don't think she realizes how lonely she is. I don't think she can hear herself think.

"Summer is great, but just wait until winter. D'you snowboard? D'you ski?"

"I'm afraid of heights," I tell her. Afraid of depths. Speed. Falling. Pain. I am the anti-RayAnn. I am afraid of everything.

She looks crestfallen, her mouth like two parentheses, a sad clown kind of face. I toss out a bone.

"But there's yoga tomorrow! I'd love to try yoga."

There are maybe twenty people in the park. In the distance, I hear children playing. Ravens as big as cats sit on tree branches, caw.

"Welcome to Laughter Yoga," says the instructor. "For the next hour I will be your leader, your guru, and your friend."

RayAnn is standing next to me. She's holding one of her feet directly over her head. With her elbow out she looks like the letter P.

"It's great exercise," she whispers. "Loosens the diaphragm. Relaxes the back."

My lips form the letter O.

"Let your mind be drawn to the spirit of the Tetons," says the instructor. "Become one with the universe." We are stretching our hands over our heads then reaching for our toes. Then waving them side-to-side like cheerleaders. I look around to see if strangers are watching because I feel like an idiot. I'm sure we look like idiots.

"Now loosen the mouth." The instructor sticks out her tongue and starts shaking her head. *Ho Ho Ha Ha Ha. Ho Ho Ha Ha Ha.* The last time I heard a person breathing that hard she was in labor. There's an old man in back of me. He's pushing eighty for sure. *Ho Ho Ha Ha Ha.* Then I hear someone hyperventilating. It's either the old man or me.

The instructor moves on to another exercise. We are holding hands in a circle, moving in, moving out. This I understand. Just when I'm getting the hang of it, she changes direction. Now the group is moving from right to left like a pile of dominoes. We are clapping on each other's backs. Banging the hell out of each other's backs. While I'm pounding on RayAnn, the old man is pounding me. Only he misses half the time. Pounding my ass, the air, my head.

"Now laugh," shouts the instructor. She forces a staccato grunt from her mouth and aims it toward the sun. "Laugh!" she commands.

I look around. Everyone is laughing. Sort of. The old man is wheezing. Some crazies are rolling on the ground holding their stomachs. When I look at RayAnn, her forehead is lined, her lips pursed. Meditation has made her incredibly anxious. She squeezes her eyes shut, fists her hands, and a series of machine gun rat-a-tats burst out. *Ho Ho Ha Ha Ha.*

"The yogina is a riot. Isn't she a riot?" says RayAnn. *Ho Ho Ha Ha Ha.* "Why aren't you laughing? Everybody's laughing." *Ho Ho Ha Ha Ha.*

I'm the only one not laughing. I've always hated smiling for the camera. It's fake sincerity. A clockwork orange. Meanwhile RayAnn is chuckling like a robotic Santa Claus stuck on someone's lawn. *Ho Ho Ha Ha Ha.*

When the group is exhausted, when sides ache and half the class has to pee, the instructor winds things up.

"Let your mind be drawn to the stillness," she says. We sit in the lotus position, knees crossed, our palms facing up, forefinger and thumb touching.

"Relax the tension. Let your spine rise from the ground. Repeat the word *So . . . ooo . . . ooo* as you inhale. Then exhale and say *hummmmm.*"

I look around for hummingbirds or bumblebees but no. It's just the sound of a dozen people collectively expelling air from their mouths. RayAnn tries so hard to relax that she looks tenser. The old man farts. The air's so still I can hear the aspen leaves whistle, the grass crunch.

And then it occurs to me. I'm the lucky one. My life's not bathed in Kumbaya but whose is? I love my husband. I worship my children. Our home is our nest. I may not have written the great American novel but I've created something of value. While everyone's quiet, I unfold like a flower and stretch. *Hummmmm.*

And then I start laughing.

There is nothing louder than a laugh at the wrong time. The instructor hisses through her teeth. Everyone in the class side-glances, sending me death ray stares. Somehow I've found a chink in their cosmic armor, put the kibosh on their karma. RayAnn doesn't speak to me the whole ride home.

We put together the local version of homemade peanut butter and jelly sandwiches and eat dinner in total silence. The goo sticks to my teeth but I can't say anything, do anything. Finally RayAnn speaks.

"While you're a guest in my home, I would appreciate if you don't make fun of my friends."

We've known each other too long for me to bullshit my way out of this. I've been hiding in a cloak of sarcasm all week. Covering my insecurities by acting superior and judgmental. And assuming that RayAnn with her *gosh darn* small-town ways wouldn't notice.

"I think you're terrific," I say. "I think yoga was terrific." I'm digging deep now. "And I really love your goats." I'm practically choking on the words. Not because I don't mean them but because my palate feels covered in mud. I stick in a finger and extract a dollop of brown sludge.

"That's disgusting," says RayAnn. Her voice is now a high shriek. "Do you know you're disgusting?"

I stick in my finger once more, circle my mouth, and extract an even bigger dollop. The relief is overwhelming. Physically. Emotionally. "Did you know this peanut butter sucks?" I blurt. "Did you know that I'd kill for a Diet Coke right now?" I pull back my finger and sling the sludge. It hits RayAnn on the stomach, two inches over her belt, and clings like a barnacle. The whole wad stays cemented to her shirt.

She looks down. She stays looking down for a long time. Then slowly she unpeels a grin. Her teeth are checkerboard. Brown. White. Brown. White. "I'd give it to the goats but they won't touch the stuff." She takes a fork, impales the brown goo that's on her shirt, and flicks it back at me. Once we start laughing, it's hard to stop.

"God, how I hate you," she says. "I hate your marriage, I hate your kids, I hate the fact that you know just who you are. You're just perfect, aren't you? I hate the way you're perfect."

She's joking. Sort of. I get up, walk around the table, and give her a big hug. "You may think you hate me but you don't."

She smiles and wipes away some tears. "You want a pizza? I know a place with great pizza."

Old friendships have a habit of sticking, too. I'm the yin to RayAnn's yang. The cream in her coffee. The perfectly timed caesura. I hang around a few extra days until it becomes an extra week. My husband and kids say they miss me. I envision a sink filled with dirty dishes and hampers stuffed with dirty clothes. It'll wait. They'll wait. The Tetons are calling. I'm one with the universe. *Hummmm.*

WE ARE NOT ALONE

FICTION

Flattened

The radio-triggered alarm mounted on the wall across the room clanged and shrieked, seizing and shocking Martha's nerves, rolling her out of bed.

Damn! Nothing for a year and a half, and it happens now? I'm getting too damned old for this.

She hauled on her jeans and a flannel shirt, yanked on yesterday's socks from where she'd unpeeled them onto the worn pine-board floor the night before, all the while gritting her teeth at the continuing ruckus. Then she pulled on her shit-kicker boots and stomped down the hallway. Her nephew Jesse should be stumbling out of the bunkroom by now. Martha pounded on his door. No response, so she shoved it open.

Jesse lay curled in a ball in the farthest of the three wrangler beds—the only one with a mattress and sheets—a pillow clutched tight over his head. Martha strode over to him, noting the open and only half-unpacked suitcase on the empty bed next to him. *What is he waiting for? He's been here two weeks and he can't make peace with being out here?*

He looked up at her bleary-eyed when she yanked the pillow away, his light brown hair sticking every which way. "What in God's name is that noise?" he moaned.

"The ley-way calling. I told you it would, sooner or later. Sorry to say it's sooner, but that's the way things are. The alarm'll keep ringing until I shut it off. Now rise and shine. We've got to get rolling."

"Rise and shine?" Jesse shouted over the racket. "What time is it?"

"About five. Just an hour earlier than I've been making you get up anyway."

Martha left, shutting the door on Jesse's groaning. She let the din go on and on until he at last stumbled into the kitchen, at which point she flipped the switch. Without the clangor, the coffee she'd started brewing in the old-fashioned percolator could be heard burbling along in a pleasant rhythm, its roasted aroma filling the air. Jesse's eyes in his thin face lit up when she passed him a filled mug.

"Drink it on the way," she said as she poured the rest of the pot into a thermos. "I slapped together sandwiches and there's another thermos filled with water. We'll eat when we get there. Now help me hook up the trailer to the Jeep."

Even in the dim, blue-gray, predawn New Mexican light, the ley-way's borders glimmered as a broad, long brand compressed into the desert floor. From Martha's vantage point looking down on it from where she and Jesse had just reset the solar-powered radio signal box hidden up on the ridge and adjusted the Jeep's rooftop solar cells to catch the rising sun, the ley-way appeared to extend clear to the Zuni Mountains in the distance to the south, though it didn't.

A month ago—the last time she'd driven by just to check on things a couple of weeks before Jesse had arrived—the ley-way had almost disappeared from sight under settling dust and drifting sand, with her traps scattered along its surface—themselves accumulating dust and sand—as the only indication of its presence.

Now, after the barrel-through less than an hour ago that had triggered her alarm, the rush of ley-way energy had subsumed dust and sand *into* the ley-way, becoming part of its dull shimmer. As had her traps.

They'd make a good haul today. About time, with money so tight. As far as she could tell, only half of her pathetic small herd of mother cows had "taken" when Carl Martinez last brought over his bull. Well, both her cows and his bull were getting old. Just like her and Carl and the other pathetic few of them still hanging on out here. And until she could afford new parts for her three windmills she wasn't producing enough power for her own modest needs *and* to sell. Then to make matters harder, Jesse arrived and she had to feed the seventeen-year-old and take care of him too.

"So that's what they look like," Jesse said, waking up at last, the wonder in his voice replacing his yawning and the way he'd been fuzzy-mumbling ever since they'd left her adobe-walled ranch house five miles back on the ridge.

"Yep," Martha said. She'd given him a hard time ever her sister Nancy shipped him down here, but she wouldn't snark him now for his obvious statement. She'd felt that same wonder when this ley-way first showed up — though terror too back in those days. And it wasn't like he'd ever had the chance to see the ley-way that transected his birthplace, Chicago. The government built a fifty-foot-high wall around the flattened and destroyed area as soon as it was able to get the shell-shocked city under control again. All of that years before Jesse'd been born. Even years before Nancy left the ranch for a hoped-for better life in the city.

So Martha nodded to put Jesse at his ease, to let him know he wasn't being boneheaded. "When a barrel-through comes blasting along scouring the surface and the whole length of the ley-way comes up shimmering from under the sand like this, it'll hit you that way. Every single time. No matter how many years you do this.

"Now let's get a move-on. We want to pull in the traps and set out new ones before the sun gets high and hot."

After they climbed back into the Jeep she put it in gear and negotiated her cautious way down through the gully to the desert floor. The open-bed trailer full of her trap-pulling gear and the next batch of traps banged along behind them.

All of her set traps stretched out in a long line on this side. No way in Hell would she ever cross over the ley-way itself and it took too damned long to drive around one end of its twenty odd miles or the other.

Even way back right after this ley-way showed up and the camps of scientists and military and whack-job cultists and other trappers damned near filled the desert on either side—even back then she never crossed at either end. Because you not only never knew when a barrel-through would come roaring along, you never knew if the ley-way might decide to lengthen itself.

Within the first few years after the ley-ways appeared around the world— steamrolling long stretches of land flatter than road kill and driving the last nail in the coffin of cooperative civilization—scientists claimed that the geological ley-line angles were fixed, their lengths stable and their widths only fluctuating within certain parameters.

Martha was of the mind, however, that something that had showed up out of nowhere from god-only-knows what other dimension or other universes could disappear or become longer or shorter or wider anytime it wanted to, no matter how stable it might seem. She had no intention of being at its business end if it lengthened and she remained cautious as all get-out as far as it maybe widening further someday.

She pulled up near the first trap, parked, opened the door and let the tell-tale after-barrel-through smell of ozone ping in her nostrils. "Don't you go near the ley-way until I tell you, y'hear?" she told Jesse. "And then you do everything I tell you *exactly* the way I say."

"I remember what you told me," Jesse said, meek as you please. Jesse had done his best to follow directions when Martha took him out to examine her windmills and ride fence on her cows. But that didn't mean Martha wouldn't keep a sharp eye on him here.

Nancy had sent her a letter informing Martha that Jesse was coming for a "visit" to get him out of the city. Said it wasn't that he was stupid—he wasn't. Nor lazy—not that either. *It's just he has a tender heart*, Nancy wrote. *He's been mugged and shaken down, but that's par for the course around here. It's the way he keeps letting himself get conned that's the problem. He's a soft touch for anybody with a sob story. I swear he has a Christ complex.*

Martha knew her little sister well enough to read the strain between lines. Besides Jesse, Nancy had two younger daughters to finish raising. If Jesse was giving things away instead of contributing . . .

A couple of years down there with you will toughen him up. Or at least let him finish growing up to be a man.

Grown men and grown women took care of their own—their families and their neighbors and those they worked with—before they reached out to others. An obvious situation out here in the wilds.

It must be worse than she'd thought in the cities if Nancy felt it better to sentence the kid to unrelenting boredom, a drought-stricken isolated parched landscape—the kind of things Nancy had fled when she'd left—and a cranky old aunt and the rarefied risk of the ley-way. But that had to be one reason

Nancy wanted Jesse here: the sheer isolation. There was nobody around to take advantage of Jesse.

The letter had left Martha shaking her head, but she couldn't write Nancy back and tell her sister no. Families *do* take care of their own. So Martha had written instead, *Fine. If there's a safe way to get him down here.* Not a lot in the way of reliable cross-country transportation nowadays, but he'd made it.

Yet now as they jacked the platform winch out of the trailer, unhooked it, and—using considerable physical persuasion—managed to drop down its cranky, pitted, corroded caster wheels, Martha considered it might just as well be that Nancy had sent Jesse here for *her*, worrying whether Martha could handle what was left of the ranch on her own any longer.

Jesse wrestled the winch's heavy solar engine into place in a matter of minutes—a task that the last few years had taken her almost a half hour.

Martha and Jesse strong-armed the winch to get it to roll about ten feet short of the ley-way's shoulder, stopping next to the first of a procession of short stubby posts that extended alongside the ley-way into the distance. The post anchored an iron hook attached to a long heavy chain that led up right to the edge of the ley-way. At which point the chain *as* a chain continued onto the ley-way as . . . something else. As a jagged, shimmery, thin, long flat something that stretched another fifteen feet into the middle of the ley-way, ending at a bigger flat shape, this one with rounded bumpy edges.

Jesse whistled, excited at reeling in his first catch. "Shall I hook up the chain to the winch now?"

"No! Not till I tell you to. Then do it *how* I tell you to. Right now just drop the winch down off its wheels and set its brakes, like we practiced back at the ranch."

While Jesse did that, Martha took her trap log out of the Jeep's glove compartment. She flipped to the current list of traps. After writing down the date at that top of that page, she noted the barrel-through's time and intensity, both recorded by the signal box. She didn't have to calculate the blast's width—the chain had transformed smack dab at the ley-way's border.

She set the log on the Jeep's hood, then nodded at Jesse. "Let's do 'er."

Together they lifted the iron hook off the post and attached it to the winch. "Remember that if you feel anything odd—anything at all—let go of the winch handle."

Jesse looked startled. "You said there hadn't been a barrel-through for over a year, but you think there'll be another one now, while we're here?"

"Most likely, no. Almost never. But it's not worth a chance." The first big barrel-through after a long dry spell often signaled a series of them rolling down the ley-way. Usually a day or two apart, but sometimes in more rapid succession.

She wiped her hands dry and put on a worn pair of work gloves. "Here's the thing. If somebody outside a ley-way is hanging onto something connected to something *on* the leyway when a barrel-through hits, that's it. You're done for."

You didn't get sucked into the barrel-through and transformed like the traps because you weren't *in* that dimension or whatever the hell it was. Instead you got smash-yanked along the intra-universe or intra-dimension border. How to get this across to Jesse so he'd take it serious?

"One of the guys who helped maintain the tents back when the government still had research camps out here said he'd seen a guy hit and dragged by a train and at least *there* some body parts stayed recognizable. But the only things left if a barrel-roll catches you when you're outside of the leyway are little gobbets of flesh, a snowstorm of tiny bone chips, and a mist of blood that floats in the air as the oddest of clouds before raining down to the ground." She pointed to the pink-orange sand of the desert floor.

"Keep in mind that the air along the ley-way gets displaced during a barrel-through—that's what the instruments record. When you feel that wave of air pressure you've got at most three seconds to let go of anything connected to the ley-way *and* get out if its way in case it gets snagged by the barrel-through."

Sobered, Jesse flipped the winch switch.

The winch's servo-mechanisms made some clunky, cranky noises before settling into a steady hum. The chain accompanied it with a clang, clang, clang as the winch rolled it up.

"Have you ever been here when a barrel-through happened?" Jesse asked while they waited for the chain to coil. "You must have at some point, you've been here so long."

"Just a few times," Martha said, her focus on the winch's progress. "Back in the beginning when I got hired on as one of the local crew members helping the researchers. I was about your age then." *Has it been that long?*

"What was it like?" Jesse prompted when she didn't say anything more.

"Like . . . nothing. One moment the world is there, the next there's nothingness—not even blackness—and you're in that nothingness, you're a nothing part of that nothingness. Then the world comes back and you with it, shaking, and little sand devils blown up from the displaced air are dancing outward on both sides of ley-way.

"Anything sitting *on* the ley-way at the time has been swept into whatever the barrel-throughs are and either completely disappeared or changed into something like this . . . " the winch had wound up as much of the chain as it could. The length of the chain no longer a chain and the object it attached to had been dragged clear of the ley-way. The former chain dangled from the last still-whole chain link on the winch like a dark strip of plastic or laminated paper, a little stiff but bendable, somewhat flexible.

"Can I touch it?" Jesse asked.

"With gloves on," Martha said as she unhooked a bolt cutter from trailer. "Don't worry. It looks fragile, but it won't break."

Jesse put his hands under the tape-like strip. "This is amazing! Where did all the space inside and between the links go? And why isn't the chain *a* chain anymore?"

Martha set the bolt cutter to the last regular link and bore down hard on the handles. One loud *snick* set the strip free to drape over the side of Jesse's hand. She poked at it with her own gloved hand.

The researchers had proved over and over that no further energy was transmitted to or from objects on the ley-way after a barrel-through, but even through her gloves she swore she could always feel *something* roiling away just beyond her fingertips. "See how inside the strip the links looked tumbled away from us farther and farther, until they fall out of sight? They're not connected because we don't even know if there's physical matter there the same way it is here, and the spaces between—all the dark charcoal gray shooting through the amber-colored shapes—we don't know if there's even a 'space' dimension, or maybe there are more space dimensions, or they're different dimensions."

Jesse flipped the strip over to examine the other side, which looked the same. "So we don't know anything? This could just be like a print photograph of the chain at the moment it got destroyed."

Martha squatted down to study at the trap itself at the end of the chain to assess its worth. "No, we know more than that. The chain *isn't* destroyed. The chains and everything else still exist on the other side. We just don't know—probably won't ever know—in what form. If form is even the right word. Think of what you have in your hand as no longer the chain, but an interface with where the chain's gone to, with what it's become. A window looking in on what the chain's become in the 'place' where it is now."

Jesse knelt beside her, studying the transformed trap at the end of the not-chain: A flattened disk with little bumps extruding all along its edge, with little bumps on the bumps, and more bumps on those. "What was it? Before, I mean."

Looked into from above, coffee and cream and caramel colored swirls shot through with glowing reddish tones and flickering blue-violets that floated over, above, and through each other in such a fully dimensional wet and liquid effect that it made Martha—who'd seen similar many a time—feel dizzy. Like always. "Give it a guess."

Jesse squinted at the object. "It reminds me of a laminated picture of a polished fossil of an ancient nautilus our science teacher passed around in class when I was in the eighth grade, sliced open to show the spiral inside. It made me think of a maze made of rooms that you could go deeper and deeper into forever, never finding the end of it. This does, too."

Not a bad analogy, Martha thought, impressed. "It was a rusted old kettle-drum barbecue." She tapped her trap log. "Just so you know before we get to them, here's what the other traps we're going to pull in today were before the barrel-through: A TV set, one of the old thick ones. A statue of the Virgin Mary—the kind they used to have in alcoves in Catholic churches before the ley-ways taught us that we didn't have a clue about religion. A bird cage. Some big bottles of a dark glass filled with the Lord only knows what. Some aluminum boxes. And a dozen other objects nobody cares a crap about anymore. At least not cares about in their original state. Don't worry about remembering all of that—I'll teach you to keep a record of everything."

They slid the transmuted object into a separate compartment of the trailer, folding its tail of transformed chain underneath it. From her collection of tools Martha unhooked a metal rod with two broad metal pads that resembled the ends of giant golf putters at each end. She swung down an attachment on the winch so that it almost rested on the ground and showed Jesse how one of the metal pads attached to it.

From the main bed of the trailer they pulled one of the many objects she'd been collecting for months—a busted ceiling fan—maneuvering it so that its undercarriage rested against the pad, its vanes spreading out above the device, which she called the "pusher." On a new page of her records log she wrote, "Trap Site #1—Ceiling Fan."

"Where do you get this stuff from?" Jesse asked. "It's all garbage."

"Anywhere I can. Sometimes old junkyards. It doesn't matter because whatever I send out there gets changed into something special and rare. The dealers and collectors don't care what it was beforehand."

Back when the various groups gathered here finally decamped, they'd left most of their stuff behind, a treasure trove for scavenging. Only the researchers had cleaned up and taken all their stuff with them. Martha hadn't had to look elsewhere for things to shove out onto the ley-way's "tarmac" for a long time. But over the years she and the other trap-setters used everything up or it rotted or blew away. Collectors still sent her some items to transform, however. Special orders. Like the Madonna statue.

She flipped a switch on the winch and the pusher telescoped outward section by chuffing section, shoving the ceiling fan out onto the ley-way inch by inch until it sat a good six feet out on the surface. Martha flipped a second switch, retracting the pusher. "And that's that. Now we pack up everything and drive to the next one."

They moved on down the line, picking up transformed objects between 200 and 300 yards apart and shoving out new ones. After a couple of hours when the sun came up hot over the hills, Jesse complained about having to jack the winch down from the Jeep and then back up into it every time. "Why don't you leave the winch attached to the back of the Jeep like it must have been in the first place?"

"Because if a barrel-through happens while we're winding a piece in, it'll drag the winch *and* the Jeep and the trailer along its vortex," Martha snapped. "Even if we survive, we'll have little shards of Jeep and winch shrapneling every which way, vaporized fluids from the Jeep's solar battery and roof array fuming up like smoke, no way to get home, nothing to show for our hard work, and no way to keep setting and harvesting traps because I don't have enough money to buy another damned Jeep."

That sobered Jesse. He didn't say a word for another few traps. Until they came to the Madonna statue trap. "What's that bump?"

Something humped up out of the flattened trap. Martha frowned. An extrusion. That could be good or bad.

They hauled it in and she breathed a sigh of relief. Like a benediction, the hands held in prayer lifted out of the flatness of the depthless beautiful mystery of the window into the other universe. The collector would probably think it was a miracle, maybe pay extra for it.

"Why is it like that?" Jesse asked. "Why didn't it flatten like the rest of it?"

"The researchers said the barrel-throughs aren't always consistent. Or maybe it has something to do with this side of things—maybe a current of air or moisture rising up off the surface, or some mineral traces in the sand that blew over and settled since I placed it here."

They hauled in a few more traps, then stopped to munch on the sandwiches, washed them down with coffee from the big thermos. Looking out over the ley-way as he ate, Jesse made the observation that it half-glittered the same now in full sun as it had when they arrived before dawn.

"Yep," Martha confirmed. "And as you'll see at some point after a late night barrel-through, it looks the same then too. Spooky at night."

"What's that little splotch out near the middle?" Jesse pointed. "It's not hooked up to a chain."

Martha squinted. Probably what used to be a scorpion. Or a tarantula. Or some-such. Hard to tell for sure from here. She calculated the distance. The pusher should be able to reach it and Jesse might as well learn about these things now.

Finishing a last swig of coffee, she got up and positioned the winch at an angle so that when she flipped the switch to extrude the scraper it passed the blotch a little to the right. Then the two of them pushed gently on the base of the extended rod so it swung over just enough to line up the pad on the far side of whatever-it-was. Martha flipped the switch. As the rod telescoped back into itself, the pusher pad became a scraper, drawing the thing across the ley-way towards them.

Turned out it was a lizard. Or had been. Jesse picked up the flat object that looked like a silhouette of a splayed fountain. But deep inside the two dimensional matrix, scales shimmered and a golden slitted eye sank and rose with the depths. Then a nictitating lid shuttered closed and open again in a quick flick. Jesse yelped and dropped the thing. "Holy crap! It's still alive in there. How can that be?"

Martha picked it up off the ground, dusted it off against her jeans and handed it to him. "It just is. That's how we know there's a 'somewhere' on the other side."

"Can't we get it back? Save it?" Jesse's voice shook.

Martha shook her head. "Don't worry. It's fine *where* it is being *whatever* it is *wherever* it is. It doesn't hurt it for us to sell its interface. Don't think of it as a lizard, but instead as a window to the other side that tracks the lizard in its new existence. "

Should she tell him it was one of the lucky ones? How many times had she checked her trap line and come across some poor critter or another caught on the ley-way at the wrong time, that hadn't been caught up all the way by the barrel-through?

A roadrunner trying to drag a flattened wing and leg, twisting itself to flop them in front of what was left of its body, trying to get some forward momentum. A scorpion with its head and one claw transformed, skittering around in circles. Nothing would come to put them out of their misery by eating them. They'd run around until their hearts gave out or the inability to eat or digest took them down. Scarce as food was in these parts, flies, beetles, wasps, even bacteria wouldn't touch them. So those parts mummified over time in the New Mexico dryness and sun, while the transformed-film parts of them that had been taken to the barrel-through universe side of things lived on forever, for all she knew.

Whenever she found them she tossed them back out onto the ley-way, hoping if they were still alive at all that they'd stay put until the next barrel-through, and that the barrel-through would come and take them all the way into the other universe. A kindness for them—not like what happened to those cult members who hadn't made it all the way. She shuddered. But those people ... Unlike the animals, they'd made a choice.

"What would happen if I hadn't seen it?" Jesse asked.

Martha shrugged. "It would have lain there until the next barrel-through. That would have swept it to the other-where all the way."

Jesse waved his arm, indicating the ley-way's width. "Why are there only your traps on this side of the road? It doesn't work on the other side?"

"It does," Martha answered. "In a little while you'll start seeing chains on that side. That's Carl Martinez's trapline. He'll have gotten a signal too, but he lives down in Grants now so he won't get here till late this afternoon, if then. He might camp out on the way tonight and pull in his traps tomorrow. He knows I'll keep an eye out for poachers today for him, but there really aren't any these days. Used to be a problem, though."

Not that all along she hadn't been keeping an eye out for a glimpse of unexpected tents and campsites up in the ridges as they moved from trap to trap.

When they arrived at her other consignment traps set out in a row—what used to be a set of boxes and the big opaque jars—Jesse had become attuned enough to notice. "Why were these the same or almost the same?" he asked after they'd winched the collapsed shapes in.

"Researchers sent them to me. Besides the per-trap fee, I get a stipend. It helps get me through lean years." *As if all years aren't lean now.*

"Why aren't the researchers still out here? Isn't this a scientist's dream?"

"It is and they were." Martha waved a hand, indicating the desert's sweep on either side of the ley-way. "This was a tent city for years, with researchers and the military trying to keep everybody else out, though they failed.

"Eventually with barrel-throughs happening only now and then and the researchers never knowing if and when they'd stop, and what with the cost of maintaining their camps—all those people sitting around doing nothing except waiting ... And why should they when those big strips of Seattle and Atlanta and Los Angeles and Cincinnati and your hometown of Chicago got barreled-through and were just sitting there with all sorts of giant-ass walls and facilities around them?

"So when the economy tanked for good and the government split apart, the researchers here had samples enough to last them a lifetime of tinkering.

They and the military pulled up stakes and left a few folks like Carl and me to trap as we please. They send us boxes and bottles of who-knows-what from time to time, I assume containing stuff based on what they've found out or not found out so far."

The rest of the run proceeded at a steady pace: Work together to haul flattened traps off the ley-way, push new traps on. By mid-afternoon, tired from the work and the sun and the wind that rose this time of day, Martha needed a real meal. If *she* felt that way, Jesse must be twice as hungry. Just a few more traps, then back to the ranch and celebrate by emptying out the refrigerator for a big nice feast.

They were about to push a new trap—a falling-apart chair—onto the leeway, when Jesse stopped, raised a finger in the air, "Hush. Did you hear that?"

Martha heard nothing but the wind. At first. Then she heard it, too.

A girl's voice, faint, calling out, "Hello? Is anybody there?"

The pit dropped out of Martha's stomach. Not now. Not ever again. It hadn't happened for years. Not since the cults fell apart.

Jesse turned around wildly, searching for the source of the voice.

Martha knew where it came from. She wanted to tell Jesse it was just a trick of the wind, but it wasn't. So she couldn't.

"Oh my god! It's coming from the ley-way. Over there!" Jesse pointed, frantic.

And there it was, further up the ley-way, almost outside of her trap line. A flattened something with a small raised surface in the middle. Something—like the lizard—not at the end of one of her chains.

Jesse ran along the ley-way to see it better, but she guessed what he'd find—a mouth. Lips. Because that's all that could explain the voice.

Jesse raced back. "It's a girl!" he screamed as he started dragging the winch alongside the ley-way.

"No, Jesse, no!" Martha tugged at him, trying to hold him back. "You have to leave her."

He shrugged Martha off, locked the scraper into the winch, swung it out at angle until it passed the object. Martha grabbed the base of the scraper to swing it back and this time Jesse shoved her. Hard. She landed on her ass, the bony bottom of her pelvis jarred by the impact. Aching, she stayed put. Fine. If it was heartache he wanted, heartache he'd get.

The shape that had been a girl was far larger than anything else they'd reeled in that day, so Jessed had a hard time scuffing her in. At one point the scraper skipped just as he was pulling on it, so it abraded across the laminate's surface and a cry of pain issued from the protruding lips.

"I'm sorry! I'm sorry!" Jesse shouted, his voice breaking into tears.

At last the scraper drew the shape in close to the ley-way's edge. To Martha's horror, Jesse leaned over the border to pull it clear the rest of the way.

Martha struggled to her feet.

"Don't you touch her!" Jesse's eyes were wild and fierce as he laid the asymmetric shape on the ground. "You'd have just left her there."

Martha sighed and nodded. "And now I can't. Don't worry about what I'll do. You're the one who hasn't done her any favors."

Jesse glared at Martha until he seemed assured she meant what she said. Then he went and rummaged around in the truck.

With her arms behind her back so Jesse wouldn't be drawn to push her again, Martha bent over the flat thing that used to be a girl. Only the mouth and jaw protruded, from an odd position at the end of the jagged asymmetric shape. The rest of the girl's facial features spiraled down and away from the three dimensional features still caught in the everyday world. The forehead floated to the left, then flipped around to the right as Martha watched. An eye emerged next to what must be the nose, then disappeared as the other eye precipitated out of an amber bubble. Looping distorted legs and arms stretched long, out of Martha's field of vision.

Martha couldn't tell what the girl had looked like—pretty or plain—but the mouth had started chapping and splitting from just these few hours in the sun, and the skin on the chin was reddening, would eventually blister and then blacken. The rest of her, however, had distorted into a graceful strange beauty, drifting in an unknowable sea of curving shapes and rich liquid colors. Martha's forehead stretched dry and tight under the flat New Mexican sun and she ached to know what the girl's eyes saw.

Jesse came up behind her, carrying the water thermos. He dribbled the water over the girl's parched lips.

"There is somebody there! Thank you! I can feel something cool on my mouth."

"Open your mouth more so you can drink," Jesse said.

Martha shook her head. "She can't hear you. Her ears are on the other side. All she can do is talk."

Jesse finally focused on Martha. "Where did she come from?"

Martha shrugged. "Who knows? She might be a last remnant of one of the cults—a kid whose mother or father came out here hoping to cross over and who either did or got hauled away by the researchers and the government. Or she could be a research student herself who came out here on her own to investigate. We'll have to look through the nearby hills to find her camp—she could have been out here for the last two weeks since I last checked my traps, or as recent as just last night. There might be something there that will let us know. And however she got herself out here."

"Are you still there?" the girl called out. "Could you touch me so I can tell you're there? Here it's so . . . more than I can say. More than I'd ever hoped it would be."

Martha reached out to tap the girl's chin, but Jesse knocked her hand away. Instead he touched a gentle finger to the girl's mouth. "I'm here," he whispered, then dribbled more water on her lips.

"If you care so much, that will make her lips burn worse," Martha pointed out. "Get her out of the sun." She opened the back door of the Jeep so Jesse could slide the shape onto the back seat. Then he fanned her through the open door with the trap log.

"Did you shade me?" the girl asked. "That feels better. You must be somebody nice. Will you help me?"

The half-digested sandwich Martha had eaten roiled in her stomach. She knew what would come next.

"I'm caught here," the girl said. "All of the rest of me is free to go, to become part of this, but I can't. Help me get all the way free."

"What can we do?" Jesse begged, now willing to look to Martha for advice.

"Do what we have to do, what we're *required* to do. Get word to the researchers and they'll send somebody for her. She's valuable now. Only a handful of cultists ended up like her, and almost none of them were left with body parts that could communicate. I only knew about one fellow who had one eye and an arm left on this side, so they had him describe what he saw with his other eye by writing it down on tablets they set up for him."

125

The military and the researchers had done everything they could to keep the cultists away, but with this long of a ley-way and in the middle of nowhere, a number of cultists always managed to sneak on at night. Once on the ley-way, nobody was going to risk going out to bring them back. They either got tired, sunburned, thirsty, hungry, or had to go to the bathroom and came back on their own accord, or they got their wish and a barrel-through took them, leaving behind flat laminates or nothing at all.

"So they can help her? The researchers can —"

"Do you have a knife?" the girl's voice from the Jeep's back seat interrupted him. "If you're all the way out here you must be a competent person who has a knife."

Jesse's hand went to the pants pocket that held the pocket knife Martha had given him the day he arrived. He pulled out the knife and looked at it.

"Here's what you have to do," the girl quavered. "It'll be hard but I know you can do it. What I'm stuck in is sort of a window or clear door. Take your knife and cut off my lips and any part of me that's sticking out of the window. Then I'll be free. It will hurt and I'll scream, but just do it."

The blood drained from Jesse's face and he dropped the knife. He looked at Martha, stricken. "I can't do that."

Martha wanted to shake him. "Of course not."

"What do I do now?"

"Like I said, she's a valuable asset and now we *have* to report her. Damn it, Jesse, I told you not to bring her in."

"But the researchers *can* help her, right?"

"I don't know what they do, but they wouldn't let her suffer." Within a day, the fellow with the one eye and arm stabbed himself in the eye with the stylus they gave him and tried to use it to saw what was left of his face off.

Jesse could tell from the look on Martha's face of the hopelessness of the situation. "What if I put her back?"

The girl couldn't hear him, but with uncanny timing she said, "Once you've freed me, put me back on the path. Then join me and we'll be float away together, free. I promise."

Martha maneuvered herself around so she could shut the open back door of the Jeep. "How could you put her back? Her lips and chin would keep burning

126

in the sun and you have no way of knowing if another barrel-through is coming anytime soon. You might as well do what she says with your knife."

Jesse got a mulish look on his face. "I could push her out there flipped over, so her face wouldn't be out in the sun."

"And scrape the hell out of her as you push her all the way out there?" If Martha could just get the door shut, then get Jesse in the front seat and drive the hell away from here . . .

"Oh. Yeah." Jesse deflated. Then he looked thoughtful. He started to close the door shut himself, then yanked it open, slamming it into Martha. This time when she went down she reached out with an arm and felt her wrist snap.

By the time she pulled herself up on her elbow, Jesse was running out onto the ley-way, carrying the girl who floated behind him like a banner, flipping it over face down even as he raced along.

And Martha knew that whether a barrel-through came along right then or not, Jesse wasn't going to make it.

WILLIAM NOTTER

We've Come to See the Fascination
—Wyoming

I'll tell you what that medicine wheel really
means. Get ready when they say that,
to hear how the Forest Service blasted out
the alien petroglyphs to hide the truth,
or local rage because the government gave in
to do-good archeologists and Indians
and locked up land that Granddad had his run of once.
Some claim sheepherders piled the rocks from boredom.
Another with a wild beard and dowsing wires
declares this used to be an oracle
but the crystals have gone silent now.

Those come too whose people's stories
know the place, or places like it,
Shoshone, Arapaho, Kiowa, Paiute,
Cherokee, Northern and Southern Cheyenne,
more than eighty separate nations,
Ute, Lakota, Blackfeet, Cree and Crow.

Many more just come: a black-fingernailed goth
from Indiana sprinkles tobacco
at the four directions, California women
ring their copper singing bowls,
bikers heading for the Sturgis rally
stomp the trail in boots and leathers,
a woman from Switzerland has her husband photograph her
lotus-style at spiritual sites around the globe.

The wiry West Virginia preacher
heard about the fascination
and brought his tight-curled wife to see.
On their way back down the mountain
he offers his conclusion. *Even primitive man*
wanted a relationship with his god.

VIVIAN WAGNER

CREATIVE NONFICTION

The Idaho Bigfoot Incident

The woman in line for tickets to the Ohio Bigfoot Conference at the Salt Fork State Park Lodge talked loudly to those around her—a flannel-wearing young couple, a sullen man in a camo ballcap, and me—about the time she saw a baby Bigfoot hit by a truck.

"I was driving my big rig on the interstate in Idaho," she said. "Right in front of me, I seen the little furry fellow run out into the road. The truck in front of me hit him. Bam! I thought at first it was a kid in his mom's fur coat, and that she would be really mad, first that he was wearing her fur coat, and then that he'd gotten himself killed."

She spoke matter-of-factly, as if her story made all the sense in the world, her snake-print polyester shirt shimmering as she talked. I listened, trying not to let on that I was undercover, that I didn't believe in Bigfoot, that I just wanted to get to know those who did. She looked at me shrewdly, like she was on to me. The more she looked at me, the more I tried to seem like a believer. I wasn't sure I was pulling it off.

"The other trucker and I brought our flashlights out and looked, but all we seen was some bloody hair," she said. "No boy in a fur coat. That's when it dawned on me that the boy weren't no boy, but a baby Bigfoot. And that a shadow I seen near the boy weren't no shadow, but a mama Bigfoot. And she must've drug that baby off into the forest before we even got there."

"Wow," flannel girl said. "That's incredible." She looked at her boyfriend, and he squeezed her hand in agreement. They'd told us earlier they were staying in a tent at the campground and had gone squatching in the woods the night before. They'd heard a few suspicious knocks and howls, but hadn't seen anything.

Snake-print woman nodded sagely.

"It was," she said. "The damnedest thing I ever seen in my life. And it's too bad, because I was headed to my first Bigfoot conference, and it would have been something to show up there and say 'Hey, look at my dead baby Bigfoot!'"

Camo ballcap guy spoke up.

"How'd you know it wasn't a bear?" he said, with the suspicious nature of a professional squatcher. You never believe any sighting until you've gotten all the facts, and preferably a footprint casting or two.

The woman laughed. "A bear?" she asked, incredulously. "Would a bear be walking up on two legs?"

He shrugged. "Yeah," he said. "I guess that's true enough."

"By God, that's true enough," she said, her blouse ruffling in indignation. "I know a baby Bigfoot when I see one, and that, sir, was one."

We were all silent for a minute, taking in the momentousness of her sighting, the tragedy that she hadn't been able to produce the corpse, the irrefutable truth of the dead baby Bigfoot. She looked hard at me.

"What do you think?" she asked.

I paused, trying to find something true to say. Because I liked this woman. I liked flannel couple and ballcap guy. And part of me really wanted to believe. I felt like I used to feel as a kid when I went to my friend's Mormon church in the California desert. I didn't know about all the Jesus stuff, and I always declined when asked for a testimony, but I sure liked the nice people, the cookies after the service, the calm coolness of the sanctuary on hot summer days.

"I think it's amazing," I said, finally. "I wish I could have been there."

R. S. GWYNN

At the Indian Casino

The loud, the proud, the well-endowed
Have come to make their mark here
Among the shuffling, gray-cast crowd
Who freely valet park here.
House drinks! And smoking is allowed!
And it is never dark here!

Each bears a plastic WampumCard
With FreePlay credits loaded,
Remembering that Cash Award
When bells and lights exploded!
No more are clinking nickels poured—
All wins computer-toted!

Long lines at ATM machines
Move forward for the taking
Of crisply measured stacks of greens
Or big bills that need breaking–
Jackson, the Red Man's scourge, the means
For dreams soon in the making:

The pleasure cruise, the gleaming car,
The bonuses progressive—
All say Chance has reset the bar
And all hopes are excessive
When economic pundits are
Predicting times recessive.

While now and then a drunken man
Is outwardly escorted
And here and there an elder can
Be heard with lines he courted
Girls with, each waitress has a plan
To keep the old goats thwarted.

The Sioux, the Crow, the Cherokee
Have planned this coming-hither
Against the ones who robbed them, the
White men who spread them thither.
They watch and smile on house tv
While hopes and trust funds wither.

Faced with no chips left in her stack,
The largish lady grumbled
That always she'd been in the black—
This time The Tribe had fumbled!
But chances are she'll soon be back—
With the quiet, the small, the humbled.

These days the tribes will never cringe
At one more Paleface coming.
In fact, no Paleface can impinge
Upon their overcoming
Demands upon such sweet revenge.
Listen to their drumming!

LARRY SCHREIBER

FICTION

Joe Shorty's Curse

One hot New Mexico Thursday in 1973, it happened. Every other day I worked as the Indian Health Service doc at Isleta Pueblo, but on Thursdays I traveled to Canoncito, a small Navajo reservation fifty miles west of Albuquerque.

I was twenty-six—at that point in my life, the reservation seemed to be a desperate place and that nothing could keep pace with the poverty, alcoholism, and child neglect.

The story had it that the Canoncitos had been scouts for the United States Cavalry and therefore scorned or at least forgotten. They were separate from the large Navajo nation, which ranged from Gallop going west and north ending in Utah. It was the size of the state of West Virginia.

At Canoncito, the Public Health nurse, Lucille Knudsen was a fifty-five-year-old lifer from Minnesota who had started working in the Indian Health Service in 1950. She was smug, bored, and condescending, but she knew every Hogan on the reservation. That day, she asked me to go on a home visit with her. We left the two-room adobe clinic, the crowded waiting room full of kids with green snot dripping from their noses, or pus from their ears from ruptured ear drums. On the wall, someone had put up a large poster of the Point Reyes Beach in northern California. It showed turquoise water, blue sky, and gold sand. The mothers of the children sat staring at the poster as we left, and as they'd been doing all day.

Going east on dirt roads punctuated by potholes capable of swallowing the 1965 Chevy government station wagon, past the landscape of hogans and trailers, we arrived at the Yazzie Hogan. Once there, Mrs. Yazzie invited me in, careful not to be rude by making eye contact. Her home/hogan was one room, with a wood-burning stove. Her husband Frank was on a bed against the curved wall, having just had a Grand Mal seizure. Mrs. Yazzie and I, eyes downcast, said nothing, but understood each other. Frank had stopped drinking forty-eight hours before. Here was the god's cruel trick on alcoholics, disregarding good intentions, or poverty, and instead adding fuel to the fire with withdrawal seizures, hallucinations, the DTs.

While examining Mr. Yazzie, it started to hail, typical New Mexico-size golf balls. Mrs. Yazzie quietly took out her broom and simply swept the hail out her doorless domain. The ferocity of the hailstorm surprised the four of us in the room: Mrs. Yazzie, Lucille, and me, along with Maria, the Community Health Representative and translator who had arrived earlier.

Translations always frustrated me. I would ask a question like "Does it hurt after a fatty meal?" Maria and the patient would talk for two minutes. Then both of them would look down; about half the time not returning with an answer. Then I would ask, trying to appear slow paced and laid back, "Well, Maria, does it hurt after she eats?" Maria would say something to the patient briefly in Navajo, and the patient would finally say, no. Translations left me in the dark, and I'd always wonder if the patient was actually answering my question, or if the two of them were saying in Navajo, "Can you believe him? He is a doctor and he gets paid for this!"

That hot Thursday, as Mrs. Yazzie swept out the hail balls, she told Maria, and Maria told me, Joe Shorty had died. Joe Shorty was a miserable human being, child molester, alcoholic, phony leader. But, Mrs. Yazzie said, "He had power. He was a very bad man. I know something terrible is about to happen. This hailstorm is part of Joe Shorty's curse." Through Maria, I told Mrs. Yazzie not to worry, that I would take care of her family despite Joe Shorty's "magic." I had to get Mr. Yazzie to the Albuquerque Indian Hospital. At that time, there was only one phone on the reservation, and it was an eight-person party line. Mrs. Yazzie didn't have a phone, or running water, for that matter.

The Canacito's clinic phone was one of the eight lines. I had to drive back there in order to call the hospital and make sure there was a bed for Mr. Yazzie. Thirty minutes later, driving the old station wagon without air conditioner, inhaling dust with every breath, I made it back to the clinic. I walked past the still waiting mothers and children, peeked at the Point Reyes picture, and picked up the phone to call the hospital.

A panicked voice broke into the party line, "A tornado has destroyed Mrs. Yazzie's hogan and has lifted the roof off Dennis Morningstar's trailer!" Dennis was a friendly, but paranoid schizophrenic, who never took his meds. Once a month Lucille gave him a Prolixin Deconate shot, a long-acting antipsychotic juice. I wondered what Morningstar imagined had happened to him: Did he believe in Joe Shorty's curse? His roof blown off by a huge wind, being isolated and being schizophrenic? I only know that Dennis was not seen or heard from for six weeks. When he showed up for his next Prolixin shot, he was calmer and less psychotic than ever.

That day I drove back to the disaster. In the rubble I found Mrs. Yazzie's granddaughter, hand outstretched, cold and motionless. This little one still had her flattened occiput from the cradle board; her mother was lying near-vomiting and weeping and complaining of numbness of her legs.

I did what I could with what I had: inserted IVs in Mrs. Yazzie's daughter, and three other injured people. Mrs. Yazzie's daughter had just lost her baby, and was in danger of dying herself. Her left upper quadrant rigid, her spleen most likely ruptured, and blood was filling her abdominal cavity. I started a second IV in her other arm to keep her blood pressure stable, and poured the saline in.

The ever-dependable Lucille drove the truck back to the clinic and called an Albuquerque ambulance; they got lost. The Laguna and Acoma EMT's did not respond. So, one hour later, I loaded four bleeding people and one dead baby into the back of my station wagon and drove to Albuquerque while Lucille held the IV bottle hanging outside of the windows. Nobody spoke or prayed (at least out loud). No one moaned. There was only me calling periodically for Lucille to give me vital signs. I drove straight to the ER at the university hospital where the trauma center was and unloaded my patients.

That night I turned on the news and learned that tornados hardly ever struck west of the Rio Grande and that forty-six people were injured. I went from exhausted to exhilarated to totally insecure. Forty-six? I'd dropped off only four injured and one dead. I imagined forty-two people buried under the rubble shouting, "Stupid white man." Was this Joe Shorty's curse? Did he, as Mrs. Yazzie had hinted, cause the tornado? There were so many things I didn't know or believe. However, when I called the ER, I learned that no one else had been hurt. The newsman had meant to say four to six injured.

I went to bed cursing Joe Shorty.

MEL GOLDBERG

FICTION

Tennis Practice

I was sixteen when my father divorced my mother and moved away from Arizona, saying he was fed up with her telling everyone she saw UFOs. The act that drove him away finally was when she claimed that one of her friends had been abducted and impregnated by aliens, who were keeping the fetus. I got a letter from him the other day. He made a joke and told me to come to Texas where the air was clean and the only aliens were the Mexican vaqueros.

I loved my mother and I believed her. She was only thirty-eight with flaming red hair and emerald green eyes, although she hated the freckles that dotted her face. I thought they were beautiful. Compared to the frumpy mothers of my friends, she was attractive and had a few boyfriends, but never anything serious.

She told me the aliens had black ships that vibrated silently, hovering just above tree tops at night, scanning for victims to abduct. Whenever someone disappeared unexpectedly, she knew who was to blame. After the divorce I had a hard time sleeping and often wasn't much interested in eating. My mother took me to doctor who said I was depressed and suffering from a traumatic stress disorder. He prescribed some anti-anxiety pills. I was afraid to take them, but my mother told me they were okay, which helped. But I was still worried about the aliens.

Every day when I took the same public bus to my high school, I saw mostly the same people. But one day at the bus stop I saw a woman I had never seen before. She wore a gray jumpsuit with long sleeves and carried an immense purse hanging from a shoulder strap. I thought it was strange because it was a hot day. I was sweating, although I wore shorts, but she seemed comfortable. She smiled at me and I got worried when she sat just

137

behind me, because there were other empty seats. She reminded me of the creatures on a TV program who were reptilian but could change their form to look like normal humans.

The bus started to move slowly through traffic and after less than a minute I heard a clicking of metal on metal. Then a swish-swish-click. I knew it was the sound of knitting. My grandmother knitted. When my mother and I visited her, she made me sweaters and scarves. So I knew the lady, or should I say creature, behind me was knitting.

But what if she knew I suspected she was an alien and the knitting was just a ruse? Aliens have a way of getting inside our brains and discovering our thoughts. Knitting needles are sharp enough to pierce skin with a forceful thrust. What if she was just waiting until the right time came to push that needle into my neck? It probably had some poison that would turn me into a zombie or something so she could whisk me back to her ship.

There was a story on TV a few weeks ago about a crazy man in Chicago who stabbed a complete stranger on a bus. The news didn't say it, but my mother and I knew the truth. The killer was an alien creature and the man he killed knew it and was about to expose him. The killer disappeared when someone tried to get him. And here I was, about to be stabbed twenty-three times in the back of the neck with a knitting needle. Twenty-three is an important number for aliens.

I put my hand over my neck, pretending to scratch it so that I wouldn't look strange. I didn't want to give her anywhere to poke her needle. I even moved my head back and forth and side to side, hoping she would find it hard to hit a moving target. My heart started beating wildly as I desperately tried to figure out a plan. I had to get out of harm's way before I ended up as this woman's tenth victim. They always do things in groups of ten.

I decided to get off at the next stop even though it wasn't mine. But I realized that's the kind of thing crazy people do, and I didn't want to appear crazy, even if it meant I was going to die.

So I sat in my seat and protected the back of my neck. But another thought struck me. What if she planned to stick that needle into my ear? If she jammed one of those things in my ear, I was a goner for sure. The poison would go directly to my brain.

I couldn't protect myself from that. I could hold my neck or move my head around, but if she was going to get me in the ear I didn't have a chance. So I spent the last few minutes of my life moving my head. I was definitely afraid. I was going to die, but maybe the other people on the bus would prevent her from getting away. She would have to stab me in front of a bus full of people. Unless the other people on the bus were other aliens. I counted them. There were twenty-three people on the bus.

Then she got up, holding the needles in her hand, and stood next to my seat, ready to strike. My heart pounded so hard my tee-shirt bounced. I took my last breath before being enslaved by a poisoned knitting needle in my ear. I hadn't even told my mother how much I loved her. The alien stood over me about to deal the fatal blow.

Then she smiled at me again and got off the bus. It was her way of telling me she knew that I knew and she could get me any time she wanted but this wasn't my time. Yet. I breathed a sigh of relief. Two stops later I got off and went home.

After that I started exercising with weights and developed strength in my chest and arms. I quit the tennis team and joined the wrestling team and did quite well. I placed third in the city high school tournament. I wanted to be prepared to fight her off the next time. Or anyone else for that matter. When I became a senior, my mother said I looked like a different person from the skinny high school kid I had been as a freshman and sophomore.

When I graduated from high school I was five feet ten inches and weighed 180 pounds. I got a job as an assistant to a manager at an insurance company, but that didn't last long. The manager was crazy. One day he told me I had to attend a sales-improvement meeting. I asked him why I needed to attend a sales-improvement meeting since I wasn't in sales. He stared at me like I was from another planet.

He told me I would never get ahead if I didn't improve my attitude. When he asked why I asked such stupid questions, I told him I didn't want to be in sales anyway. I probably should have kept my mouth shut, but the next day I quit and started an online course to become a physical trainer. A month later I got a job at a health and fitness club as a trainer. The pay was not great, so I had to continue living with my mother.

From the fitness center where I worked I could watch young women playing tennis.

They were slim and athletic and I suspected some of them might be aliens in disguise. The ones I knew weren't aliens were good looking. I was never very good at meeting girls, and I thought playing tennis again might help me meet some of them. I had to be alert because I didn't want to become the victim of an abduction. I could tell aliens by their unusual smell. That was something they couldn't hide, even when they used a strong deodorant.

I bought an expensive racquet. Although I had played in high school, I never played very well.

There was a practice wall near the courts and I went there by myself. For my birthday, my mother bought me an inexpensive video camera and a tripod to film my moves. She said that was the kind of thing that professionals do to see how they might improve. That sounded good because I didn't want to look foolish in front of the girls.

My mother came to watch me practice one afternoon, and when she heard the pop of the tennis balls against the wall, she said it sounded like the landing of the alien ship that had abducted her friend. She said she had heard the same popping sound as it sucked her friend up into their ship. She had not seen it because the ship was invisible, vibrating at a speed too fast for the human eye. She emailed ufo.com and told them what she knew. She had emailed them many times before but they never responded. She was afraid of being abducted and having her body taken over and the last thing she wanted was to get pregnant. I understood her fear.

After she videotaped me, she played the video back in slow motion. She had read an article online that stated our eyes miss things in the speed of reality, unlike the aliens or bees or flies who see things as they really are with their compound multi-faceted eyes. Bees can see pollen in a flower from hundreds of feet away. Flies can detect movement and are so fast most people miss them with fly swatters. I thought watching the videotaping at a slow speed was a good idea.

I wanted to see my arm movement to make sure I was watching the ball and swinging my racquet from low to high to get top spin. We watched the videos carefully hoping it would help me to improve my swing.

* * *

Did you ever catch a furtive movement out of the corner of your eye and when you turned to look, nothing was there? That happens to me a lot. One day, as I tossed the ball up to practice my serve, I caught a movement out of the corner of my eye. It was a low-flying bird, and in a reflexive action, I swung at it and caught it in mid-flight, killing it. I felt terrible, but it was probably an alien spying on me. The entire scene had been captured on video.

That evening I watched it with my mother and when we slowed the action down she said she could see a slight vibration in the air behind the bird, like the wake made by a boat. We stopped the video at the instant my racquet struck the bird and she claimed she saw the ghostly hint of a grotesque reptilian face as the bird's spirit departed.

My eyes were not trained as well as hers and I thought it might have been a slight vibration of the camera caused by the wind. I played the video for several days in my room, studying it carefully. Last night I saw the face, too.

ALINE KAPLAN

FICTION

Voices in the Dark

I could tell from the sound of her footsteps on the stairs that the Duchess was in a bad way.

The steps were light, as she was a small woman, but slow. She took a while to reach the hotel lobby, and by the time her feet hit the last step, I was in place and ready. Offering the Duchess my arm, I supported her on the short walk to one of the stiff horsehair sofas. Tears streaked her face and she wore an air of resignation, almost defeat, that I had never seen before. The Duchess—Annabella McGarrick by name—was a strong woman and one who handled the rough men and demanding customers of a frontier town with aplomb.

That meant the voices had been particularly bad.

I went to the kitchen door, glad to have something solid to do instead of just holding her hand while she cried. Sing Lee was stirring a huge pottery bowl of sourdough starter. He looked up when I came in, a question in his narrow black eyes.

"Tea," I said shortly. "And make it strong." Sing Lee nodded sadly, chunked some pine kindling into the wood stove, and moved the kettle over it. He knew the routine as well as I did. Sing Lee muttered in Chinee as he spooned fragrant oolong into the teapot and I heard the word "gwai-lo." I knew that "white ghost" was what a Chinaman called white people but I think he meant the real kind, the spirit kind, instead. Sing Lee filled the pot with hot water and set it on a tray along with two mugs and some sugar.

He checked the icebox and said, "No milk. Come in morning."

"That's fine," I said, taking the tray. "She won't notice."

I backed through the door into the lobby and carried the tray over to the little marble-topped table in front of the sofa. By this time the Duchess was sitting upright as a piano, clutching something in her lap as though it was the crown jewels. She was wearing a wool wrapper and her hair, braided for the night, made a streak of gold on her left shoulder.

The Duchess was not a beautiful woman. Her face was too round, her brows too heavy, her mouth just a little too wide, but I always enjoyed looking at her, even when she was in a state she called "dishabille." She had an education and the graces of a lady for all this was the ragged edge of the frontier. I poured tea into both mugs, leaving an inch of mine empty. Going to the bar, I added a splash of whiskey from the moderately good bottle to fill it up. Dealing with a weeping woman required sustenance stronger than a tea leaf could offer.

I sat beside her on the sofa and waited. The nights had turned cool in the mountains and the warm crockery felt good in my hands. Slowly, the Duchess let go of a small notebook with a brown leather cover and put it nearby on the sofa. She picked up her mug of tea and looked at me through the steam. Over the past two years I had learned to hold my piece and wait until she was of a mind to speak. So we sat in silence for a while until she said, "The voices came again. You understand, Jake?"

I nodded.

"They were strong, loud. At first I just lay in bed and listened, hoping that I would finally understand who the ghosts are and what they want."

She sipped her tea. I wished that I could have put some whiskey in hers too, but the Duchess had no truck with liquor of any kind. She said it stole one's wits and she needed hers about her at all times. Given what I knew of her life, I couldn't disagree.

"But what I heard was not usual," she continued, "Just—more so. There were strange words that didn't make sense and letters put together that sounded like words but could not be so."

"What was different?" I asked. We had had these talks before, and I tried not to show my opinion of ghosts. My demons were all of the flesh-and-blood kind, but spirits that talked at night were real to her.

The Duchess sniffed and sat a little straighter, if that were possible. "On a normal night—if I can describe any of them as normal—the voices are more like murmurs or whispers in the dark. I can't rightly make out what they're saying, you understand."

"Have you tried speakin' with 'em?" I asked. "To find out what they want?"

She nodded and took a sip of tea. Those deep blue eyes looked at me over the rim of the cup. "I have tried everything, Jake. I have asked them questions, quoted scripture, even threatened them with my scattergun once or twice, although I'm not proud to admit it, but nothing has had any effect. They are just spirits, after all. I have come to understand that the voices don't talk to me, only to one another. I tell them to go away and to leave me alone, and sometimes they do seem to hear me, but they never listen. They never do what I ask."

Her hands clutched the mug so tightly I feared that she would break the sturdy Palace Hotel crockery in two. "It's like eavesdropping but frightening. Sometimes I rise and turn up the lamp to try and scare the ghosts away."

"I have heard that ghosts don't like light," I said, as though I was talking about a real threat, like wolves.

She nodded. "I leave a lamp on low in my sitting room all night like a mother would for a child who is afraid of the dark. She set her cup down and clasped her hands in her lap. "My rooms are haunted. I am a grown woman, a widow, a person of means and importance in this town, but tonight I was as frightened as a little girl."

"That sounds right sensible to me," I said. "No one can see your lamp and I surely won't tell."

She smiled at that, just a small lift of those soft lips. One day I would . . . I took a slug of tea and shook off those thoughts. Mrs. McGarrick was my employer and that was all. If she knew of my past, she would not welcome my advances and certainly reject any tender of affection. Hellfire, she might just throw me out in the street. I pulled myself back to what she was saying.

"Usually the voices are indistinct. They fade in and out as though the speaker were going to and fro in the room—or leaving it and coming back. Tonight, well, they were stronger, as though the men were closer or more powerful."

"Men? Are they always men?" My attitude improved right away; I know how to deal with men. She shook her head. "The ghosts can be either men or women. Most times, I can't tell at all—they're just whispers. But tonight they were definitely men."

"What did they say?"

144

The Duchess set down her cup and took the notebook. "I have been writing the voices down for a while," she said. "At least, what I could hear or understand well enough. Tonight I filled pages until, not to put too fine a point on it, I fled." She offered the book to me. "Read it, Jake. You'll see what I mean." I accepted the notebook, and with a small sigh, as though she had let go of a great burden, she lifted the teapot and filled our cups again.

The notebook was ordinary enough, lined paper bound in tan calfskin with the words 'McGarrick Company' stamped in gold on the front. I had seen one like it often enough in Frank McGarrick's office next door to the hotel. He had used them to record transactions, noting the size and weight of gold nuggets given as payment along with silver, U.S. and Canadian Dollars, Spanish Reals, Mexican pesos, and bartered goods. This one bore none of Frank's bold scrawl so I knew the Duchess must have taken it straight from the shipping box.

I had not liked Frank "Duke" McGarrick above half when he was alive. Not because he was a strong man who had taken what he wanted (that's what's required to survive out here), nor because he used his sharp mind to outwit other men who were slow of thought, frantic to get out to the gold fields, swallowed by debt, or desperate for any of the reasons that landed one in a mining town. It was because he liked it.

Don't get me wrong, I'm no angel, but I did the things I have done because I had to, while Frank had seemed to enjoy getting the better of others—and squashing them flat when he could. I destroyed bodies with my guns but he ruined lives with his power. That joy in the destruction of human souls is what I objected to. Still, to give him his due, he had taken good care of the Duchess and never stepped out on her that I or any other man knew of. He hadn't even touched the whores he ran out of the Golden Stake saloon on the other end of Main Street.

Now a widow, the Duchess still lived at the hotel—for the noise and the company she said, although I suspected that memories were more important—and listened to voices in the dark while the rest of the town was sleeping.

I could almost smell Frank McGarrick's cigar smoke when I opened the book and set myself to parse it. Reading does not come easy to me but I did not want to display that lack to Annabella. Entries on the first pages were brief and somewhat of a kind. The Duchess wrote in a delicate feminine hand. The script was clear and I found it easy enough to get the sense of her words. She had used a bold letter M or W to indicate, I reckoned, whether the speaker was a man or a woman. Most of the voices sounded almost like hotel guests who were looking for something, exclaiming in surprise or calling to someone to show herself. I didn't like the sound of that one bit at all.

There was no real sense to the fragments, especially as some of the words were, as the Duchess had said, unrecognizable. They were surely not American. In my youth I picked up some Spanish and added a few phrases of Apache when I was on the run. I even got some Chinee words from Sing Lee, although I would not let any white man know that. But these sounded nothing like any of those languages; there were letters I understood, but they were put together in ways that made no sense at all.

I turned to the last pages she had written, the ones from tonight, and saw with some relief that the words were clearer and the sentences were more complete. Two men were talking about a task they had set themselves to do and it seemed to involve putting up equipment — except that the machinery they were using was not something I had ever heard of. I was reminded of Shorty Phelan, the telegraph man, when he talked about how they ran the lines out alongside the railroad tracks and how the dots and dashes worked. Shorty was smarter than I am and had studied. He understood the thinking behind telegraphy and the description of it made sense to him but damned if I could grasp how it all worked.

I turned to the last page and my hair stood on end. The words were unmistakable with that bold 'M' in front of them: "Duchess, are you there?" My mouth went dry. These weren't just conversations overheard in another room,, they were talking directly to Mrs. McGarrick. The tea in my cup was cold, but hell, most of it wasn't tea anyway. I slugged it down, welcoming the whiskey's sharp bite in my throat. The liquor was hard and strong and it steadied me. I kept reading.

M: "Can you hear us?"

A bold letter 'A' appeared as my Duchess talked back to them. I felt a burst of pride. She might make herself out to be timid but she was as brave as any cavalryman.

"What do you want?" she asked back.

M: "Did you hear that?"

M: "Yes, yes, I've got it."

A: "Who are you?"

M: "My name . . . Gary."

M: ". . . I'm Josh."

A: "Well you can just get out of my room."

M: "I couldn't hear . . ."

M: "No dude . . . on the . . . ee vee pee . . . clear."

M:". . . talk to us . . . Duchess. Why . . . here?

I looked up at her. "They're not just voices anymore, are they?"

She shook her head. "No, they used my name. They want me. That's what it signifies. It's what has rendered me so frightened. I tried to speak with them—you can see that."

I nodded.

"I thought perhaps, if I knew what they wanted, I could persuade them to leave me alone. But then, it all overwhelmed me. I was talking to ghosts in the middle of the night in the dark. Even with the lamp on, I was frightened. I had to leave."

"I can understand why you would," I said.

"Yes." Her voice was bleak. "Who might these spirits be, Jake? The Palace is not very old and Mr. McGarrick and I have always lived in the top suite. I can assure you that no one has ever died in it."

I shrugged. Such speculation was beyond my experience. While death and I are well acquainted, any spirits that might visit this world have left me alone.

"Do you think it might be . . ." she began cautiously and stopped.

"No, I do not," I said firmly. "Your husband is at peace and, at any rate, would not do such a thing." By all accounts—and there were more than a few—Duke had died surprised and before his time out on a claim he had just taken from its starving owner. Word had it from those present that he had turned red and clutched his chest. With a strangled "Ooof" he had dropped to his knees like a pole-axed steer and then toppled onto a stream bank. His body had been cold and stiff by the time they got him back to town where the doc told us what was already clear to be seen.

Many a man had felt cheated of his revenge the day Duke McGarrick died facedown in the mud, but I wasn't one of them. He had left Mrs. McGarrick well provided for. She was a rich woman and I had no doubt that he lay quiet in his grave—at least in regard to Annabella.

She nodded in agreement. "I just don't know what to do, Jake."

I said nothing. I wanted to help but I had no idea how to go about it.

"Would . . . you go up there?" she said in a small voice. "I know it's a terrible imposition to ask this of you. I hope that you will excuse my presumption but I am at my wit's end."

"Go to your room? Ma'am, I would never be so bold . . ."

She waved her hand to silence me. "I understand your reluctance. But no one need know. After all, we're not in Boston or Philadelphia. I thought maybe you could hear them, too. And if you could, it might even be possible to, well, scare them away."

"*Me* frighten *them*? How?"

Her eyes, huge and blue and serious, locked on mine. For a moment I stopped breathing.

"You've done things in your life, Jake. I don't know what those things were and I don't want to know but I have observed how other men behave around you. They do not stand close to you or trifle with you and they are careful of their words. That tells me a great deal." She shook her head and the tears welled up again. "I know it's a lot to ask and it may not accomplish anything but would you do it? For me?? Please?"

I cannot say whether it was the tears or the pleading, but there was no way I could refuse her. I nodded. Rising from the sofa, I stepped behind the hotel desk and took up my holster and gun from the shelf where I kept them in easy reach. Hotels have money and Black Rock, Colorado, was still a raw town. Strapping on the belt, I went to the bottom of the stairs and started up.

The gun felt heavy and friendly on my hip, like an old dog that had come to my side as I went out to fight. I liked the heft of it and the way it made me feel young again and strong. With each step I waited for my danger sense to kick in and warn me, but nothing happened. Still, when I strode down the hall and opened the door at the end, my heart hammered as though I was going up against a real opponent. That was nonsense. The word "dude" had been written clearly in Annabella's book, which meant they came from some city back east and weren't likely to be a real threat. Closing the door behind me, I looked around to see if anything suspicious might make itself known. Mrs. McGarrick's two-room suite was large, and the parlor was lit by a gas light, turned down low, on the back.

"Is anyone here?" I asked. A buzzing noise came as my only answer. It was like the low hum of a beehive but one that was far away. It set my teeth on edge.

I moved cautiously through the parlor to the bedroom. It smelled of her scent, something flowery. The buzzing sound was louder here, harsh, and my danger sense lifted the hair on my arms. That feeling had kept me alive in times and places where I could have—and maybe should have—died, and I trusted it. The gun was out of its holster and in my hand before I could think about it.

In the next room, I saw the lamp on a table near the large bed that, rumor said, had been shipped out from back East at great cost. Its dark, carved wood headboard loomed against the wall. Swallowing, I looked away from the rumpled sheets that were probably still warm from her body. In such a feminine place, I felt like a longhorn bull in a millinery shop.

Dismissing that thought, I ordered myself to get down to business. I drew breath. "Who's here? Step out where I can see you."

There was no response. I took up the lamp and went from corner to corner in the room, looking for God knows what. I saw a spider web in one corner, women's clothing on the long chair, and fripperies on the dresser, but that was all. Despite what my sense told me, the room was empty. I pivoted slowly, looking at every detail, waiting for something to move in the edge of my eye. I felt like a damn fool waving a loaded Colt around an empty room . . . and a lady's bedroom at that. That's no way to handle either a gun or a lady. Besides, how do you aim at a ghost?

Well, I had to do something, didn't I? Finding nothing, I pondered what to do next. If I couldn't hear the voices, I could not remove whoever made them, but I could at least warn them off.

Drawing in a deep breath, I stopped my gabbling thoughts, made myself still and spoke. "My name is Jake Ranscomb. Men who have reason to know that name know to tread lightly around me." I stopped and waited. "You may not fear me but hear me out."

Silence. A breeze stirred my hair even though the windows were shut tight; the air shifted around me as though someone invisible was moving in the room. My mouth went dry and I wanted another slug of that whiskey but I had told Annabella I would do my best, and I could not be less brave than she was. Besides, the night was cool and windows are drafty things.

"I know you're just ghosts," I said. "I know you can't touch her or hurt her, but you *can* frighten Mrs. McGarrick, and you have done so. I cannot allow it. You must go away. Now. Go and leave Annabella alone."

Only the hum replied. It was unnerving and I am not a man whose nerves rattle easily. "Talk to me, damn you," I said, my voice rising. "If Mrs. McGarrick can hear you, so can I. Say something!"

But the ghosts would not talk to me. Perhaps they knew something about me that rendered them mute. Perhaps it was something I did not know about myself, although that seemed unlikely. I had spent too many nights thinking about who I was and what I had done in my life to have any false ideas. Holstering my Colt, I waited awhile, standing still as a marble statue and listening to that infernal hum. Finally, conceding defeat, I walked out and closed the door behind me. I could protect my Annabella from any man living and would consider myself lucky to give my life for hers, but I was helpless against the dead, at least for now. It made me feel less of a man to know that and I did not like that feeling one little bit. Someday I would join those spirits and then I would find the ones who had frightened the only person in the world who meant anything to me.

Then we would have us a time.

"Did you get all that?" Gary asked. "What a great session!" He snapped on the lights and the nineteenth century hotel room appeared in all its renovated and refurbished glory. When people were asked to pay extra to stay in a haunted room, they wanted atmosphere, and The Palace Hotel's new owners in Macau had spared no cost to provide it.

"You bet," Josh said." "It's the best recording we've ever done, and I think we'll get even more on the EVP when we play it back in the studio."

"The Duchess herself. Wow. I mean, I thought we might get some good readings, but I never thought that we would actually, like, hear her speaking."

Josh shrugged. "Well, dude, it *is* the haunted suite after all. I guess that *Ghosts of the Old West* had it right when they called it the most haunted place in Colorado."

Gary did a little victory jig as he rolled up the cable, his double chin jiggling. "When we put this up on YouTube it's going to, like, go viral. Thousands of views, man. Maybe hundreds of thousands. This can put us in the big time." Smile beaming in a round rosy face, he moved faster than people seeing him for the first time expected.

"Weelll," Josh drawled, "I don't know about that. Let's not go overboard." He paused and then shrugged. "But it sure beats anything any of the ghost-hunting programs have broadcasted all year." Josh lined up the mics and started putting them away. His lank pony tail swung as he swiveled from table to case.

"We got the Duchess on tape, and in HD, too. And it wasn't just a random message playing back. We got a response. She was talking to us."

"That's what the guests who have heard her all say, though, even if she is just telling them to get out." Gary laid down the last coil of cable and snapped the case shut.

"Maybe not, but we do have a solid recording." Gary turned and surveyed the room. "Cameras next?"

"Sure," Josh replied. "I'll get the ones in the corners."

"And that other voice," Gary said. "What did you think of that?"

Josh stretched his tall frame, pulled down a night-vision camera and handed it carefully to Gary, who laid it in its case and closed the lid. They moved to the next corner. Josh did not reply until he had that camera in hand. "I don't know," he said. "It was definitely a man, though."

"It might have been old Duke McGarrick himself," said Gary as he stowed the second camera away. With all the equipment shut off, the room was still and silent.

"Anything's possible, dude," said Josh, hands on hips. "But we won't know for sure until we listen to the EVP."

"No," Gary conceded. "But he sure sounded threatening."

Josh smiled. "Maybe so. You should know by now, though, that ghosts are just energy manifesting from the other side. Duke McGarrick, the Duchess, all of them died over a hundred and twenty years ago. We can hear them and sometimes they can hear us. But they can't hurt us. Now let's pack this all up and get out of here. I'm tired."

"Yeah, and I'm hungry. Let's get something to eat."

"Tomorrow we'll put it up on YouTube. Then we'll just stand back and wait for the views to start rolling in.

"It's going to be good, dude. Real good."

The two men picked up their cases and left the Duchess' room, closing the door carefully behind them.

DON KUNZ

Take My Hand

I'm hand picked, hand carved,
Hand painted, hand cranked,
Hand sewn, hand thrown,
Hand blown, hand crafted.
I'm a handmade handful.
I can be a farm hand, trail hand,
Gun hand, helping hand.
I can handle your handout,
Handbasket, handbag, handcuff.
Hands up, hands down, hands off,
I'm on hand, handy, handsome.
I can be your right-hand man.

Mine's a good hand, a glad hand;
It's a hot hand, a poker hand.
It's the hand I've been dealt.
I come to you hat in hand,
Not high handed or heavy handed.
And if you choose hand over fist,
I will walk with you hand in glove,
Past left-handed compliments.
You can eat out of my hand.
Don't bite this hand that feeds you.
It could have a bird in it.
I offer this hand in marriage.

There is no sound
Of one hand clapping.
So, let's join hands.
Show your hand.
Take my hand.
Be my handmaid.

RENÉE THOMPSON

FICTION

Recovery

Shiloh was a lean dog with sparse black hair and the sitting-stance of a cheetah. When the hover first dropped her off in the high desert of southeastern Oregon, she had walked on all fours, searching the parched earth for the scent of humans, their scat and urine and toilet paper, which they crammed under rocks and hid behind bushes, and which the wind tossed down the highway. The next morning, she stood upright, her long narrow muzzle shifting and shortening, so that it now resembled a nose. By the third day her transition was complete, and so she rummaged through the small nylon bag she carried with her, donned shoes and a skirt, a short-sleeved blouse, and a wig that covered her ears.

She needed no map or instruction to locate the drug-rehab center, situated in the scraggly juniper forest of Jackdaw Mountain. The building was a squat, single-story structure made of gray cinder block and single-pane windows, a porch that wrapped around. The commissioners had possessed the good sense to approve construction in the rural, largely unpopulated county, where, if a resident took a notion to abandon the program, there was simply nowhere to go.

The center provided twenty-four hour live-in services and treated patients addicted to alcohol, OxyContin, Percocet, Vicodin, heroin, cocaine, methamphetamine, Xanax, ecstasy, LSD, Valium, PCP, and Ketamine—more commonly known as Special K. Shiloh knew about Special K, as the drug had been administered to her firstborn pup, after Hugo Saxton hit it with his car.

The center's manager hired Shiloh the day she walked through the door. "It's our good fortune you wandered in," said the woman. "It's hard to find help in Clark County."

From ten p.m. to six a.m., Shiloh worked as a janitor, mopping floors, scouring toilets, and emptying trash from the residents' rooms. Each evening, after she'd finished polishing the mirrors in the women's restroom, she sat outside, top of the steps, to grieve and gaze at the stars. The other workers attributed the habit to snobbery, assuming that because Shiloh preferred to spend time alone she was too good for them, when she was merely preoccupied, watching for the brilliant blue flash in the western sky that told her the craft was coming. Once it landed, she'd have exactly four minutes to kill Hugo, the night watchman—to bite his throat, rip open his chest, and bolt down his heart and liver. That deed completed, she would walk from the center, morph into her preferred dog state, and calmly board the hover.

Hugo kept an eye on her. She felt his gaze on the back of her neck, and when she turned to look at him, he made no effort to look away, just kept his eyes fixed on hers, having no sense at all that to stare was a threat, and would get him into trouble.

One night, after she'd finished her shift, she was sitting on the steps, scanning the horizon. Hugo opened the door and stood at its entry, the silhouette of his body illuminated by the recessed lights in the hall. He was a big man in a blue uniform, hands the size of bull's hooves. Twice she'd seen him slip Oxy to the woman in 13A, taking with those hands whatever he wanted, his eyes daring Shiloh to tell. But she didn't tell, she kept quiet. Knowing her time would come.

Hugo spoke to her back. "Wondering how you come and go," he said. "You got no car, there ain't no bus. No one drops you off."

"How I travel is none of your business." Hugo wasn't used to such talk from a woman, and she sensed his jaw clenching.

"You sit there like you're somebody," he said, stepping forward, "but you ain't nobody, hear?"

She turned her head and issued a low, guttural growl. She heard him hesitate.

"You're a sick son of a bitch, you know that, lady? They ought to lock you up."

The night Hugo hit her pup with his car, he didn't stop, or slow, or turn around to see what he'd done, just pressed his foot on the accelerator and drove hard toward tomorrow. Shiloh's firstborn lay on her side on the tar-ribboned asphalt, until a passerby stopped to help her. The man, an old rancher who'd seen plenty of sick and dying dogs in his day, couldn't abide suffering, and so he loaded her into the back of his pickup and took her to his vet. "I'll pay whatever it costs," he said quietly, "just do what you can to help her." She hung on all night and most of the next morning, but died in the afternoon.

Shiloh ached for her firstborn. It wasn't right, what Hugo had done, and just because he lived here and she lived there—because he was human and she was not—didn't mean justice shouldn't prevail. And so she watched and was careful and took no time off, and when she saw the blue-vein streak break the evening sky, she let her tongue fall between her canines, pulled off her wig, and shivered up her hackles. Two minutes later, Hugo was no more than a few tattered shreds of a white uniform, a bloodstain on the floor. And when Shiloh boarded the hover, she dropped to all fours and sat like a cheetah. Gazed out the window as the craft took off and the planet grew small, and paper tumbled across the highway.

CONTRIBUTOR NOTES

Contributor Notes

Bredt Bredthauer is a poet, touring cyclist, and professor of English. He earned a BA from the University of Texas at Austin, an MA from the University of North Texas, and an MFA from the University of Florida. After completing his MFA in 2012, Bredthauer gave away all his worldly possessions and embarked on a multi-year solo bicycle tour around the world. He crossed over thirty countries and three continents while living in a tent and relying entirely on the kindness of strangers. Currently, Bredthauer is living and working in Saudi Arabia.

Bartholomew Brinkman is an assistant professor of English at Framingham State University, where he teaches courses on expository writing, American literature, and modern and contemporary poetry. In addition to his scholarly writing, he has poems published or forthcoming in the Evansville Review and Salamander.

Amy Brunvand is a librarian, activist and compulsive writer in Salt Lake City, Utah. Her publications range from scholarly articles to book reviews to cranky letters to the editor. She writes regularly for *Catalyst Magazine* ("Resources for Creative Living") mostly about environmental issues and dancing. Her recent poetry appears in, *Journal of Wild Culture, Canyon Country Zephyr,* and *Dark Mountain.*

George David Clark is the author of *Reveille* (winner of the Miller Williams Prize) and teaches creative writing and literature in the honors college at Valparaiso University. His most recent poems can be found in *Alaska Quarterly Review, The Believer, Blackbird, Yale Review,* and elsewhere. His work appears reprinted at *Verse Daily, Poetry Daily,* and in a variety of anthologies and special series.

Michael Luis Dauro lives in Bloomington, Indiana, where he works, writes, tutors at an after-school program, and mentors incarcerated writers. He has been named a 2014 Millay Colony resident artist, and was a finalist for the 2013 Ruth Lilly Poetry Fellowship. His poems have recently appeared in *At*

Length, Golden Key, Sonora Review, As Us Journal, Luna Luna Magazine and *Rattle*. He is a Ten Club member and a CantoMundo fellow.

Carol V. Davis is the author of Between Storms (2012). Twice a Fulbright scholar in Russia, she won the 2007 T.S. Eliot Prize for *Into the Arms of Pushkin: Poems of St. Petersburg*. Her poetry has been read on NPR, Radio Russia and at the Library of Congress. She is poetry editor of the *Los Angeles Jewish Journal*.

Russell Davis has written and sold numerous novels and short stories in virtually every genre of fiction, under many pseudonyms. He has also worked as an editor and book packager. A past president of the Science Fiction & Fantasy Writers of America, he currently teaches in the Genre Fiction MFA program at Western State Colorado University.

Joe DiBuduo and **Kate Robinson** love weird fiction. DiBuduo sports the vivid imagination and Robinson wields the revision toolbox and the word-whacking polish. DiBuduo is the author of a novel, *Cryonic Man: A Paranormal Affair* (Tootie-Do Press, 2015), and *A Penis Manologue: One Man's Response to The Vagina Monologues* (CreateSpace, 2009), a nonfiction narrative. Robinson is the author of a novel, *Heart of Desire: 11.11.11 Redux* (Tootie-Do Press, 2014), and two history books for middle-graders (Enslow, Inc., 2005 & 2010). The story "Cheater" made its world debut here and will appear in *The Contest*, an upcoming collection of connected stories inspired by famous paintings.

Michael Engelhard is the editor of *Wild Moments: Adventures with Animals of the North* and author of *Where the Rain Children Sleep: A Sacred Geography* of the Colorado Plateau. He works as a wilderness guide in Alaska but has not driven a car since 1989. Trained as an anthropologist, he can eat viscera while keeping a poker face.

Daniel Ervin is a full-time undergraduate student of Writing and Religious Studies at Rockhurst University in Kansas City, Missouri, and a part time barista in a local coffee shop. He has previously called both Omaha, Nebraska, and Varanasi, India home, and his poetry often struggles to integrate the landscapes and culture in which he grew up with the religious realities of the larger world. "The Buddha's Geology" is Daniel's first published poem.

Mel Goldberg writes every day, plays tennis three days a week, and is active in writers critique groups. He earned an advanced degree in literature and taught in California, Illinois, Arizona, and Cambridgeshire, England. He and his wife and sold most of their possessions and traveled in a small motor home for seven years throughout the U.S., Canada, and Mexico.

R.S. Gwynn is the author of several collections of poetry, including *No Word of Farewell: Selected Poems 1970–2000*; *The Narcissiad* (1982), a book-length satirical poem; *The Drive-In* (1986), winner of the Breakthrough Award from the University of Missouri Press; and *Dogwatch* (Measure Press, 2014). is the editor of *Poetry: A Pocket Anthology* (2001) and *New Expansive Poetry: Theory, Criticism, History* (1999). He has also edited two volumes of the *Dictionary of Literary Biography*. His poetry has been featured in many anthologies and textbooks.

Aline Kaplan has been writing science fiction for many years and has published two novels: *Khyren* and *World Spirits*. Her short stories appear periodically. She has been a member of the Science Fiction and Fantasy Writers of America since 1988 and the Spacecrafts Writing Group since 1995. Her blog The Next Phase (AKNEXTPHASE.COM) covers a variety of topics. She lives in Hudson, Massachusetts.

Don Kunz taught literature, creative writing, and film studies at the University of Rhode Island for thirty-six years, retiring as Professor Emeritus. His essays, poems, and short stories have appeared in over seventy literary journals. He lives in Bend, Oregon, where he writes fiction and poetry, volunteers, studies Spanish, and is learning to play the Native American flute.

Nate Liederbach is the author of the story collections *Doing a Bit of Bleeding* (Ghost Road), *Negative Spaces* (Elik), and the forthcoming three collections, *Blessings Galore* (Wordcraft of Oregon), *Tongues of Men and of Angels: Nonfictions Ataxia* (sunnyoutside), and *Beasts You'll Never See* (Winner of the 2014 Noemi Press Book Prize for Innovative Fiction). He lives in Eugene, Oregon and Olympia, Washington.

Ellaraine Lockie is a widely published and awarded author of poetry, nonfiction books and essays. Her eleventh collection, *Where the Meadowlark Sings*, won the 2014 Encircle Publication's Chapbook Contest and was published in early 2015. Ellaraine teaches poetry workshops and serves as Poetry Editor for the lifestyles magazine, *Lilipoh*. She is currently judging the Tom Howard/Margaret Reid Poetry Contests for Winning Writers.

Nathan Alling Long's work appears in over fifty publications, include *Tin House*, *Glimmer Train*, *Story Quarterly*, and *Crab Orchard Review*. He is currently seeking publication for his story collection, *Everything Merges with the Night*, as well as a collection of flash fiction, *Fifty-Fifty*. Nathan lives in Philadelphia and teaches creative writing at Stockton University in New Jersey.

Robert Garner McBrearty's stories have been widely published, including in the Pushcart Prize, *North American Review*, *Missouri Review*, and *Narrative*. He's published three short story collections, most recently *Let the Birds Drink in Peace*, Conundrum Press, and a forthcoming novel, *The Lonesome Western Society* (Conundrum). His writing awards include the Sherwood Anderson Foundation Fiction Grant.

Teresa Milbrodt is the author of a flash fiction collection, *Larissa Takes Flight: Stories*; a short story collection, *Bearded Women: Stories*, and a novel, *The Patron Saint of Unattractive People*. Her short stories, flash fiction, and poems have appeared widely in literary journals. Milbrodt teaches online fiction and creative nonfiction classes through Denver-based Lighthouse Writers Workshop. Read more of her work at TERESAMILBRODT.COM.

Lance Nizami has no formal training in the Arts. He started writing poetry during a long airplane flight in late 2010. As of 1 March 2015, he had 144 poems in print or in press (not online), the most recent acceptances being at *94 Creations* and *Maintenant*.

William Notter is the author of *Holding Everything Down* (Southern Illinois University Press), winner of the 2010 High Plains Book Award for Poetry and a Colorado Book Award finalist. He grew up in northeastern Colorado and holds an MFA from the University of Arkansas. His poems have appeared on the *Writer's Almanac* and in journals including *Alaska Quarterly*, *AGNI*, *Crab Orchard Review*, *High Desert Journal*, *Midwest Quarterly*, and *New Madrid*.

Born in Brooklyn, raised in Miami, and educated at the University of Michigan, **Marlene Olin** recently completed her first novel. Her short stories have been featured in publications such as *Emrys Journal, Upstreet Magazine, Biostories, Vine Leaves, Poetica, Edge,* and the *Saturday Evening Post* online. She is a contributing editor at *Arcadia*.

C. R. Resetarits has new poetry in *Hawai'i Review, Worchester Review,* and *Pacific Review* and new fiction in *MacGuffin* and *China Grove,* all out late spring/summer. Her poetry collection, *Brood,* will be published in 2015 from Mongrel Empire Press. She lives in Faulkner-riddled Oxford, Mississippi.

Michaela Roessner has published four novels and shorter works in publications including *Trop Magazine, F&SF, OMNI, Room Magazine* and assorted anthologies. Her novel *Walkabout Woman* won the Crawford and John W. Campbell awards. She's had pieces short-listed for the Calvino Prize, Tiptree Award, Mythopoeic Award, and Millennium Publishing contest. She teaches at Western Colorado State University's MFA in Creative Writing Program.

Larry Schreiber M.D. has lived and practiced medicine in northern New Mexico for thirty-nine years and serves as Hospice Medical Director for Mountain Home Hospice of Taos. Schreiber worked as a medical team leader for the International Committee of the Red Cross on the Thai-Cambodian border in 1980. His upcoming journal publications include *War, Literature and the Arts, Anak Sastra, Lime Hawk Literary Arts Collective, Dirty Chai, No Bullshit Review,* and *Eastern Iowa Review.*

Matt Schumacher has authored two poetry collections, *Spilling the Moon* and *The Fire Diaries.* A chapbook, *favorite maritime drinking songs of the miraculous alcoholics,* will be published this summer. His work has recently appeared in *Grain* and *Chattahoochee Review.* Poetry editor of *Phantom Drift,* he lives in Portland, Oregon.

Renée Thompson is the author of two novels, *The Plume Hunter* (Torrey House Press, 2011) and *The Bridge at Valentine* (Tres Picos Press, 2010), which was selected as the 2014 community book for Woodland Reads. Her stories have appeared in *Crossborder, Narrative, Literal Latte, Arcadia, Chiron Review,* and elsewhere.

David J. Rothman directs the Graduate Program in Creative Writing at Western State Colorado University, the program's Poetry Concentration, its conference "Writing the Rockies," and its journal, *THINK*. Recent books include two volumes of poetry, *Part of the Darkness* and *The Book of Catapults*, and a collection of creative nonfiction, *Living the Life: Tales from America's Mountains and Ski Towns.*

Wendy Videlock lives on the Western Slope of the Rockies in Whitewater, Colorado. Her work has appeared widely, most notably in *Poetry, Hudson Review, American Arts Quarterly*, and the *New York Times*. Her newest book, *Slingshots and Love Plums*, is available from Able Muse Press.

Vivian Wagner is an associate professor of English at Muskingum University in New Concord, Ohio. Her work has appeared in *The Kenyon Review Online, Zone 3, McSweeney's, The Pinch*, and other publications. She's also the author of *Fiddle: One Woman, Four Strings, and 8,000 Miles of Music.*

Kirby Wright was the 2014 Writer in Residence at the Earthskin Artist Colony in New Zealand. *The Girl With the Green Violin*, his poetry chapbook is due out in Spring 2015. Look for his memoir set in the islands in late 2016.

About the Editors and Designer

Mark Todd is Editor-in-Chief at Western Press Books and this year exercised executive privilege to also serve as editor for the current edition, *Manifest West #4, Western Weird*. He's taught at Western State Colorado University since 1988 and served as director of Graduate Studies in Creative Writing at Western from 2010 until 2014. Author of two collections of poetry, *Wire Song* (Conundrum, 2001) and *Tamped, But Loose Enough to Breathe* (Ghost Road, 2008); the science fiction novel *Strange Attractors* (Write in the Thick, 2012) ; co-author with wife Kym O'Connell-Todd of the paranormal comedy Silverville Saga trilogy, consisting of *Little Greed Men* (2011), *All Plucked Up* (2012), and *The Magicke Outhouse* (2013)—all from Raspberry Creek Books; and the creative nonfiction book *Wild West Ghosts* (Raspberry Creek Books, 2015), also co-authored by Kym O'Connell-Todd.

Laura Anderson is a writer and editor for the *Gunnison Country Times*, in which she has published countless articles. She is the editor of the *Gunnison Country Magazine*. She holds a Bachelor of Arts in English as well as a Certificate in Publishing from Western State Colorado University. Laura spends her weekends writing and exploring the beautiful Colorado valley she calls home.

Jennifer L. Gauthier has a B.A. in Letters, which covered the topics of language, writing, literature, philosophy, and history from the University of Oklahoma and a publishing certificate from Western State Colorado University. She recently completed an internship with the Montrose (Colorado) *Daily Press*. Her love of writing began at age 9, and she recently produced her first novel, *Among the Threads of Time* (self-published in 2014). Currently she is completing and editing her second novel.

A.J. Sterkel has a B.A. in English from the University of Colorado Denver and a publishing certificate from Western State Colorado University. Before working as an associate editor for *Manifest West*, she worked as an editorial assistant for *Copper Nickel Literary Journal*. She is an MFA student in the Writing for Children and Young Adults program at Spalding University. She lives in Colorado and is writing a young adult novel.

Larry K. Meredith is former director of the Publishing Certificate Program at Western State Colorado University and served in the position of editor for *Manifest West #3, Different Roads*. He previously served as Western's Assistant to the President and Director of Public Relations. He has been a newspaper man, a salesman, an advertising and sales promotion writer for a Fortune 500 company, director of a library district, and has owned his own marketing and video production firm. He is the author of the historical novel *This Cursed Valley* (2012) and has another novel and a biography with a literary agent. His publishing company, Raspberry Creek Books, Ltd., was formed to publish books that "celebrate the American West."

Sonya Unrein is a freelance editor and book designer. She has a master's degree from the University of Denver in Digital Media Studies, and lives near Denver with her husband and cat.